Using Photography and Other Arts-Based Methods with English Language Learners

Using Photography and Other Arts-Based Methods with English Language Learners

Guidance, Resources, and Activities for P–12 Educators

Edited by
Tabitha Dell'Angelo
Louise Ammentorp
Lauren Madden

ROWMAN & LITTLEFIELD
Lanham • Boulder • New York • London

Published by Rowman & Littlefield
A wholly owned subsidiary of The Rowman & Littlefield Publishing Group, Inc.
4501 Forbes Boulevard, Suite 200, Lanham, Maryland 20706
www.rowman.com

Unit A, Whitacre Mews, 26-34 Stannary Street, London SE11 4AB

Copyright © 2017 by Tabitha Dell'Angelo, Louise Ammentorp, and Lauren Madden

All rights reserved. No part of this book may be reproduced in any form or by any electronic or mechanical means, including information storage and retrieval systems, without written permission from the publisher, except by a reviewer who may quote passages in a review.

British Library Cataloguing in Publication Information Available

Names: Dell'Angelo, Tabitha, 1970–, editor. | Ammentorp, Louise, 1972–, editor. | Madden, Lauren, 1980–, editor.
Title: Using photography and other arts-based methods with English language learners : guidance, resources, and activities for P–12 educators / edited by Tabitha Dell'Angelo, Louise Ammentorp, Lauren Madden.
Description: Lanham : Rowman & Littlefield, 2017. | Includes bibliographical references and index.
Identifiers: LCCN 2017025845 (print) | LCCN 2017040631 (ebook) | ISBN 9781475837636 (electronic) | ISBN 9781475837612 (cloth : alk. paper) | ISBN 9781475837629 (pbk. : alk. paper)
Subjects: LCSH: English language—Study and teaching. | Arts in education. | Photography in education.
Classification: LCC LB1576.5 (ebook) | LCC LB1576.5 .U85 2017 (print) | DDC 372.6—dc23
LC record available at https://lccn.loc.gov/2017025845

∞ ™ The paper used in this publication meets the minimum requirements of American National Standard for Information Sciences Permanence of Paper for Printed Library Materials, ANSI/NISO Z39.48-1992.

Printed in the United States of America

During this book project, several of us lost loved ones suddenly.
This book is dedicated, with love, to their memory
Alma Rosario
John Tyler Dell'Angelo
James P. Meyers Jr.

Contents

Preface ix

Acknowledgments xv

1 Engaging English Language Learners through the Arts Using the Aesthetic Overlay of CRISPA 1
Donna Goodwin and P. Bruce Uhrmacher

2 Sensemaking through Art Making: Trash for Teaching and Visual Arts Integration with Elementary Emergent Bilingual Students 17
Kristin Papoi

3 Photo Elicitation: Using Photography with Elementary ELL Students 29
Carissa Natalewicz

4 Becoming a Community: How an Arts-Integrated Curriculum Supported the Development of English Language Learners in a Kindergarten Classroom 39
Rebecca Garte and Michelle Allen

5 Telling Stories after School: Using Photography to Build Literacy and Community 51
Tabitha Dell'Angelo, Lauren Madden, and Maureen Hudson

6 Bilingualism and Project Arts-Based Learning 59
Laura Felleman Fattal

7 Photovoice as a Vehicle for Supporting Environmental Literacy and Language Acquisition 69
Marissa E. Bellino, Jennifer D. Adams, and Joanna Higgins

8 Exploring Identity through Image: E-Portfolios Supporting
Cross-Curricular Learning for English Language Learners 83
Sarah Morrison

9 The Selfie Project: Using Photographs to Improve Writing with
Diverse Learners 95
Browning Neddeau

10 Who Are You? I Am . . .: Activist Art to Author ELL Identities 105
Sheron L. Mark

11 Everyday Photography Tips for Your Classroom 117
Destiny De La Rosa

Index 123

About the Editors and Contributors 129

Preface

The purpose of this book is to provide educators with guidance, resources, and activities for incorporating arts-based approaches into their classroom practice. The chapters are written by practitioners who have successfully implemented the strategies and activities with English language learners (ELLs) in the classroom. Chapters describe projects from a variety of grade levels and disciplines. Each chapter presents innovative ways to engage students in high-level, high-quality work.

Our intention is to offer practical classroom ideas that are theoretically grounded. Each chapter contains resources, sample plans, and student work. In addition, the theoretical background and up-to-date literature review in each chapter provides readers with important references should they choose to apply for grant money or formalize these ideas as part of their school or district curricula.

The authors have provided examples from multiple content areas and grade levels. Some chapters offer a focus on historically underserved communities in the United States. Additionally, two chapters share work with an international focus.

Although each chapter takes a unique approach, they each include the following:

- A research- or theory-based discussion of how and why this methodology works with students
- Activities, lesson ideas, assignments, material lists, and so forth, that are easy for the reader to follow
- Suggestions and recommendations for the K–12 practitioner
- Resources such as books and websites
- Student work samples or other relevant images

In addition, we have a special section dedicated to easy-to-use photography tips that are designed for a classroom setting and can be taught by anyone, regardless of photography experience.

WHY NOW?

According to the National Center for Education Statistics (2016) the percentage of English language learners in public school in the United States was higher in school year 2013–2014 (9.3 percent, or an estimated 4.5 million students) than in 2003–2004 (8.8 percent, or an estimated 4.2 million students) and 2012–2013 (9.2 percent, or an estimated 4.4 million students). Lesli Maxwell (2017) reports that the Pew Research Center is projecting that by 2050, 34 percent of children in the United States under the age of 17 will "either be immigrants themselves or the children of at least one parent who is an immigrant."

This reality presents a challenge for a teaching force that continues to be relatively monocultural. Among more than three million public school teachers, approximately 82 percent are non-Latinx white; fewer than 10 percent are non-Latinx black or Latinx (Ross et al., 2012). To be sure, nonnative English speakers are not all Spanish speakers. However, the Latinx population is growing most rapidly.

These demographic realities between the teaching force and the student body create a challenge for teachers trying to bridge the cultural gap. And while all aspects of culture are important, language presents challenges that need to be mediated to support student learning.

LEARNING ENGLISH IN AMERICAN SCHOOLS

Most sources suggest that students take anywhere from four to seven years to master academic English. Much of that variation is dependent upon their English-proficiency level when they began schooling in English (Cook, Boals, & Lundberg, 2011). Students with limited English proficiency have very different levels of support. In some schools and districts, they are in a self-contained English as a second language (ESL) classroom for part of the day; in some cases an ESL teacher "pushes in" for some instruction. But in almost all cases, nonnative English speakers are in a typical classroom for at least part of the day. That requires all teachers to implement strategies to support these children.

The strategies suggested in each of the chapters of this book can be implemented by "general education" classroom teachers without special training in ESL. This can provide additional supports and opportunities and present multiple avenues for engaging ELLs throughout their school day.

ARTS-BASED METHODS ALLOW STUDENTS TIME TO PROCESS AND MEANING-MAKE

The use of arts-based pedagogy has been used to build literacy skills across content areas, using objects that can be held and manipulated to teach history (Fuhler, Farris, & Nelson, 2006). Kay Cowan and Peggy Albers (2006) promote the idea of using arts-based methods to develop strong literacy practices. Beth Olshansky (2008) uses pictures to teach writing with great success. The chapters in this book offer concrete ways for children to engage with materials. These methods support their ability to develop more complex ways of thinking and knowing. Providing students the opportunity to "see" text is a methodology that is valuable for all students but can be particularly useful for students who are learning a new language and are having to use and interact with that language in multiple ways. Additionally, the time required to make decisions about how to represent ideas artistically offers some space for children to negotiate ideas and develop meaning.

Often school-based ESL programs are heavily focused on vocabulary. To be sure, learning a new language and a lot of content-specific vocabulary can be daunting. Support in this area is important. Still, while some children are growing their vocabulary, others are learning how to interact with those concepts and apply and connect these ideas. The works created using arts-based instruction can serve as connectors, allowing children to express their ideas more completely than with words alone—discussions around these works can lead to more robust conversations about children's ideas and allow them to practice using vocabulary at the same time. It is important to find ways in which English language learners can both build their vocabulary and have opportunities to apply and grow their critical-thinking skills.

THE SOCIAL, COLLABORATIVE, AND CULTURAL IMPORTANCE OF THE ARTS FOR ELLS

Contributors to this book offer a variety of suggestions for arts-based instruction with ideas that require collaborative creation, discussion, and analysis of works. This emphasis on collaboration provides yet another avenue for building skills in ELL students. When children have the opportunity to identify a visual feature or pause at a particular musical phrase, they can literally pinpoint details worth discussing and writing about. ELLs and native English speakers alike can hone in on details in a way that often can't be done without a strong, shared, working knowledge of the language. The arts also support ELLs to authentically interact and build relationships with their peers in a context that is not language dependent.

The uniqueness of arts-based pedagogies can offer an engaging change of pace for all students. Activities like the ones described in our chapters provide new experiences for all learners—ELLs and native English speakers alike. Having the chance to work through new challenges is a shared experience that can lead to camaraderie among students from a variety of cultures and backgrounds. Over time, the students will develop a shared expertise and increased confidence both in their abilities to engage in arts-based learning and in navigating the dialogue in the classroom.

As Luis Moll (1990) discusses, the purpose of education from the Vygotskian approach is to "help children appropriate and take control of their own learning and develop strategies for understanding the social world" (p. 13). From this perspective, learning is understood as a social process, and the school setting should provide students with strategies and knowledge to assist them in their everyday lives. The arts, and photography in particular, can help students bridge the gap between home and school, helping teachers understand student lives while assisting students as they learn about world around them (Ewald & Lightfoot, 2001). This is particularly important for ELLs who, in addition to learning English, are also learning about American culture and schooling.

USING THIS BOOK

An important feature of this book is that anyone can use it. Regardless of whether you have training in working with nonnative English speakers, you will find the ideas useful and easy to follow. And you do not have to be an artist or photographer to integrate these ideas into your classroom. The book is designed for anyone to be able to implement ideas as described or to use parts and create new activities and ways to interact with material. These ideas can be integrated into a traditional classroom setting or as part of an extracurricular program. There is even a chapter with easy-to-use photography tips that can be used by people of any skill level.

As general education teachers take on more responsibility for accommodating children with different needs and learning preferences, new ideas are always important. And the ideas in this book have all been used successfully. We felt it was important to share ideas from real teachers who have worked with real children and found these methods effective. We hope that you will share your stories with us. If you try something out that you found in the book, please let us know what worked, what didn't, and how you made it your own. Building a community of educators who are all working to share ideas, support one another, and rejoice in shared successes is incredibly important. Share your stories by e-mailing ellartsbook@gmail.com.

REFERENCES

Cook, H. G., Boals, T., & Lundberg, T. (2011). Academic achievement for English learners: What can we reasonably expect? *Phi Delta Kappan, 93*(3), 66–69.
Cowan, K., & Albers, P. (2006). Semiotic representations: Building complex literacy practices through the arts. *Reading Teacher, 60*(2), 124–137.
Ewald, W., & Lightfoot, A. (2001). *I wanna take me a picture*. Boston: Center for Documentary Studies in association with Beacon Press.
Fuhler, C. J., Farris, P. J., & Nelson, P. A. (2006). Building literacy skills across the curriculum: Forging connections with the past through artifacts. *Reading Teacher, 59*(7), 646–659.
Maxwell, L. A. (2107). U.S. school enrollment hits minority-majority milestone. *Education Week, 34*(1), 1, 12, 14–15.
Moll, L. C. (1990). Introduction. In L. C. Moll (Ed.), *Vygotsky and education: Instructional implications and applications of sociohistorical psychology* (pp. 1–27). Cambridge: Cambridge University Press.
Kena, G., Hussar, W., McFarland, J., de Brey, C., Musa-Gillette, L., Wang, X., Zhang, J., Rathbun, A., Wilkinson-Flicker, S., Diliberti, M., Barmer, A., Bullock Mann, F., & Dunlop Velez, E. (2016). The Condition of Education 2016 (NCES 2016-144). U.S. Department of Education, National Center for Education Statistics. Washington, DC. Retrieved Dec. 2016 from http://nces.ed.gov/pubsearch.
Olshansky, B. (2008). *The power of pictures: Creating pathways to literacy through art, grades K–6*. San Francisco: Jossey-Bass.
Ross, T., Kena, G., Rathbun, A., KewalRamani, A., Zhang, J., Kristapovich, P., & Manning, E. (2012). Higher education: Gaps in access and persistence study (NCES 2012-046). U.S. Department of Education. Washington, DC: National Center for Education Statistics.

Acknowledgments

First, a thank-you to the divine influence of social media that led our editor, Sarah Jubar, to a little blog about using photography with English language learners.

From Tabitha: Thank-you to Alfonso Llano for being a tireless advocate for the children in his school and to Mrs. Rios for always going above and beyond to let her students know how much she cares. These educators and others like them who approach teaching as an act of love have an enduring influence on hundreds of children throughout their careers.

Special thanks to my coeditors and friends without whom this book would not have happened. And finally, thank-you to my wonderful husband, Steve, and my two little squirrels, Ben and Joey. They put up with the "button-eye mommy" popping up from time to time during this project and supported me anyway.

From Lauren: Thank-you to all the classroom teachers and teacher educators who warmly welcomed us into their classrooms by sharing their work. We are especially grateful to Jeanne Muzi for her thoughtful input in the midst of a crisis. Thank-you to my coeditors for inviting me to join your team and think deeply about these important strategies, and for being outstanding friends and colleagues. Lastly, thank-you to my loyal husband, Mike, and loving boys, Connor and Luke. Any task that ends with your smiles is worth doing.

From Louise: Thank-you to all of the authors for sharing their knowledge and experience. Thank-you to Lauren and Tabitha for being the best coeditors, colleagues, and friends a person could ask for. And thank-you, Keith and Kaya, for letting me work when I have to and making me laugh when I need to!

Chapter One

Engaging English Language Learners through the Arts Using the Aesthetic Overlay of CRISPA

Donna Goodwin and P. Bruce Uhrmacher

USING THE ARTS TO HELP *ALL* LEARNERS SUCCEED

Finding ways to engage students and encourage agency in their learning is a priority for most schools. Students with limited language proficiency, however, present additional challenges. Without a focus to address the specific needs of English language learners (ELLs), many students are at risk of losing educational opportunities provided to students generally. This chapter examines one elementary school as it incorporates elements of a sheltered language instruction protocol (National Center for English Language Acquisition [NCELA], 2015) combined with arts and aesthetic considerations. In this chapter there are examples of how classroom teachers are reaching learners, specifically ELLs, by using CRISPA, an acronym for an arts-based aesthetic overlay that includes Connections, Risk-taking, Imagination, Sensory experiences, Perceptivity, and Active engagement in planning and instruction. It is our hope that educators will be able to take these examples and strategies and apply them to their own unique situations.

During the past school year, one of us worked with teachers and the staff from Sherman Elementary,[1] located in a small town in the foothills of northern Colorado, on ways to incorporate elements of sheltered instruction into the school's curricular focus on arts integration. Sheltered instruction is an approach that emphasizes grade-level content while also providing for language proficiency. Sherman Elementary is designated a Title I school and has a population of approximately 300 students, grades kindergarten through fifth. It is a part of a district-wide program consisting of an elementary, middle, and high school that provides curriculum designed to integrate visual and performing arts across content and meet the needs of a variety of learning styles. The teachers at Sherman Elementary wanted a way to combine best practices of meeting the needs of their ELL students with their focus on arts integration. However, they did not want to abandon their current teaching practices and curriculum, and they did not want to add an entirely new approach to their already overloaded to-do lists. Using the aesthetic overlay of CRISPA along with strategies from sheltered instruction models became a solution for this school.

HOW DOES THIS COMBINATION WORK? THE BRAIN AND ELLS

Howard Gardner's *Multiple Intelligences* (2006) defines intelligence as human "cognitive competencies" or a set of "mental skills or intelligences" (p. 6). He argues there are eight different types of intelligences that all humans possess with varying degrees of strength depending on the individual: visual-spatial, musical, bodily-kinesthetic, interpersonal, logical-mathematical, intrapersonal, linguistic, and natural. We note Gardner's theory here to suggest that ELLs may seem to have weak linguistic intelligence when in reality it may simply be that they cannot speak or read as fluently as a native speaker. They may very well have a high linguistic intelligence in their native languages.

In his book, *How the Brain Learns* (2011), David Sousa points out that the brains of some learners may not be as responsive to the sounds of a nonnative language. Therefore it is important that additional areas of the brain, "other than those associated with linguistics," be engaged to help with language acquisition using multiple intelligences and multiple modalities (p. 193). There are many sociocultural and psychological factors at play when acquiring a second language and learning new content simultaneously. This chapter focuses on commonalities among successful language acquisition models and the aesthetic learning strategies of CRISPA that helped the teachers and students at Sherman Elementary.

ARTS INTEGRATION AND STRATEGIES FOR ELLS

Integrating the arts into the everyday curriculum is a focus for Sherman Elementary. By doing this they hope to build experiences and background knowledge for students in order to link future learning. They also bring in community arts partners and artists as well as take students to arts centers for field trips. They have been able to show increased attendance among students and increased parental involvement since this focus began. Sherman is also a Title I school, and the school district in which Sherman Elementary is situated encourages the staff to attend professional development in sheltered instruction to benefit not only the school's population of second language learners but also all students.

One type of organization of learning for ELLs is called "cognitive apprenticeship" (Gibbons, 2009, p. 33), which consists of four main components:

- learners participate in "rich," real-world-like tasks;
- thinking is made visible;
- observation plays a key role: learners are given opportunities to observe models of a task as a whole prior to attempting to execute it; and
- abstract tasks or tasks involving low-level skills are situated in authentic contexts, so that students understand the relevance of what they are doing (Gibbons, 2009, pp. 34–36).

Another popular model for making context and language comprehensible for ELLs is called Sheltered Instruction Observation Protocol (SIOP). It has eight components: preparation, building background, comprehensible input, strategies, interaction, practice/application, lesson delivery, and review/assessment (Echevarría, Vogt, & Short, 2012). These in turn are divided into smaller features such as using visuals, making links, making learning meaningful and authentic, using dramatic and oral rehearsal, and grouping and collaborative work, among other ideas. Teachers and staff members at Sherman use strategies from cognitive apprenticeship and SIOP—and they wanted a way to layer their focus on arts integration with the sheltered instruction they are already doing. CRISPA became a simple way to do so.

WHAT IS CRISPA?

CRISPA is an acronym for the dimensions of an aesthetic experience, an approach that has been researched since the late 2000s and first published in 2009 (Uhrmacher). This research was initially conducted by observing arts-based professional development institutes where teaching artists worked with practicing teachers. The themes that were uncovered by watching artists were then checked against the ideas of John Dewey (1934) as found in his book *Art as Experience*.

In the end, six dimensions of an aesthetic experience were identified and elaborated upon (Uhrmacher, 2009) to provide a means for students to engage authentically in a learning experience. The six are connections, risk-taking, imagination, sensory experience, perceptivity, and active engagement. CRISPA is not intended to be a model for any specific type of content area or for a given type of student; rather, it is a means to attain engagement and deeper understanding, a way to "turn ordinary learning experiences into aesthetic ones" (Uhrmacher, 2009, p. 614).

Stated differently, when one undergoes an aesthetic experience, a kind of "wow" experience one may have in nature or when engaged in the arts, the six themes just mentioned are enacted. Therefore, if teachers can help bring these themes in their teaching, they increase the possibilities for students to have engaged learning experiences. The themes may be utilized as an overlay to any given curriculum. Moreover, the themes of CRISPA align well with and enhance those of quality instruction in language acquisition.

HOW CRISPA STRATEGIES BENEFIT ELLS

Connections

By fostering a sense of connection between the student and the content in a lesson, the teacher provides the students with a way to truly relate to the subject matter. The connection could be intellectual (something that is interesting to the student), communicative (a connection to a person, place, or time period), emotional (a visceral response to the subject matter [Moroye & Uhrmacher, 2009]), or social (a feeling of involvement due to the social nature of engaging with the content or activity [Moroye & Uhrmacher, 2012]).

Connections are particularly important for ELLs as it allows students to begin learning new language or content based on existing knowledge (Peregoy & Boyle, 2008). It creates a sense of buy-in and motivation to learn and allows for scaffolding of information, self-direction, and a sense of purpose. Connections also fold into the SIOP model of learning (Echevarría et al., 2012) in many of the eight components, but in particular the area of background building to make links between established and new concepts.

Risk-Taking

It could be argued that a small amount of risk must be involved to truly learn anything of consequence (Uhrmacher & Bunn, 2011). With ELLs, risk is important in learning, but it is also important that there is not so much risk that a sense of safety or self-preservation staunches the desire to acquire new experiences. Because of this tension, providing safe spaces for risk-taking is a key element in working with ELLs. This can be done by establishing routines and schedules that provide a sense of security for all students (Peregoy & Boyle, 2008), but it is especially important for those who are new to the language and culture. Collaboration and group work are also ways to help build in safe risk-taking for ELLs, and they fit into SIOP interaction component (Echevarria et al., 2004) seamlessly.

Imagination

One way to utilize imagination with ELLs is to use the cognitive apprenticeship method of allowing students to observe a new technique or concept before attempting it on their own (Gibbons, 2009). This gives students time to imagine the possibilities of what their own participation will be and look like. Another way that imagination is important to ELL experiences is that it allows for end products to be open ended and as complex as the student can envision it; imagination can take a variety of formats or creative outcomes to show and demonstrate knowledge. As Christy Moroye and Bruce Uhrmacher write in their 2009 article "Aesthetic Themes of Education," "The use of the combination of active engagement and imagination provides opportunities for students to take control of their learning in something novel or even extraordinary" (p. 94).

Sensory Experience

Experiencing a new idea or concept through multiple modalities and senses is especially important to ELLs. It allows varied ways to understand and can provide connections that build to greater knowledge. Experiencing through multiple senses also provides a means of repetition of experiences that can be context embedded (Peregoy & Boyle, 2008), making learning more attainable. Using cultural products such as music or foods from native cultures can also create connections and a sense of belonging for ELLs and can also provide opportunities for sensory and emotional connections to new content (Moroye & Uhrmacher, 2010).

Perceptivity

Perceptivity is an important aspect of ELL acquisition of knowledge. In order to grasp a new language or concept, students need to slow down and experience the new idea or concept completely. If learners' first interpretation does not make sense, they need to go back and reexperience the situation until it does. This is particularly true for learning to read and write in a second language (Peregoy & Boyle, 2008).

Active Engagement

In many cases ELLs are actively engaged because they have real and immediate life needs that are motivating them to learn (Peregoy & Boyle, 2008). An example could be wanting to choose the right flavor of snack at the lunch line or needing to understand what new friends are saying in order to play a game. Pauline Gibbons relates this as situating new learning into authentic situations to show relevance. Additionally, when students are physically and actively engaged, they are learning through multiple intelligences, which create strong connections in the brain (Sousa, 2011).

CRISPA IN ACTION IN THE CLASSROOM

First-Grade Stories

Sharon Scoggins and Jane-Ellen Loren wanted to start the new school year building a sense of community in their first-grade classes. Knowing that their English language learners grasp novel concepts best when new information builds on background knowledge, they decided to teach community traditions and focus on the connections that can be found in varying examples of students' family experiences. They chose the guiding question "What is a community?" and planned using the CRISPA graphic organizer (see figure 1.1) to be sure they included elements that could engage students more deeply in the content. They highlighted where sheltered instruction overlapped with CRISPA. Sharon and Jane-Ellen used the CRISPA Lesson Sketch format (see figure 1.2) to plot the lesson components that culminated with an art activity in which students created a collage representing their understanding of community traditions.

Description of the Lesson

Sharon and Jane-Ellen began the lesson by gathering photographs taken from the Internet of family and community celebrations such as birthday and anniversary parties, quinceañeras, weddings, and holiday-themed gatherings. After showing each photo, they encouraged the first graders to think-pair-share, to look at and consider the image, and then to turn to a partner and discuss their own stories and understandings about the images.

Studies reveal (Applebee, Langer, Nystrand, & Gamoran, 2003; Arreaga-Mayer & Perdomo-Rivera, 1996) that ELLs typically spend very little of the school day speaking in their second language, and even less of that time involves academic content. By providing this visual prompt and an opportunity to talk, the teachers were encouraging students to use their language skills with a safe amount of risk-taking that incorporates elements of CRISPA and SIOP. Sharon and Jane-Ellen let their students do most of the talking throughout the entire lesson and cut time spent lecturing down to a minimum. They described how their students learned a great deal about each other in these conversations and began to show greater empathy toward each other as well. Sharon shared a story to illustrate this claim. When one student told the others in his group he had never had a birthday party, the group later came to the teacher, told her how sad they felt, and then asked to secretly plan a class party for his next birthday.

Engaging English Language Learners through the Arts 7

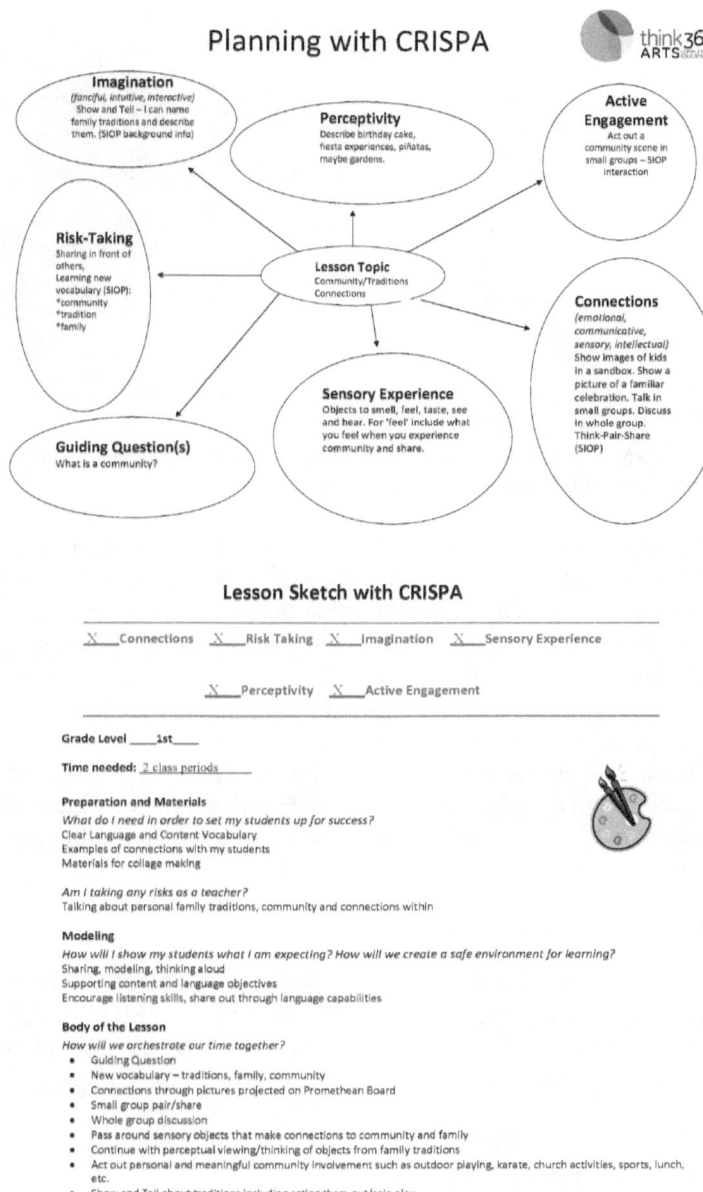

Figure 1.1. Example of first-grade CRISPA lesson sketch and graphic organizer.
Photo by Donna Goodwin.

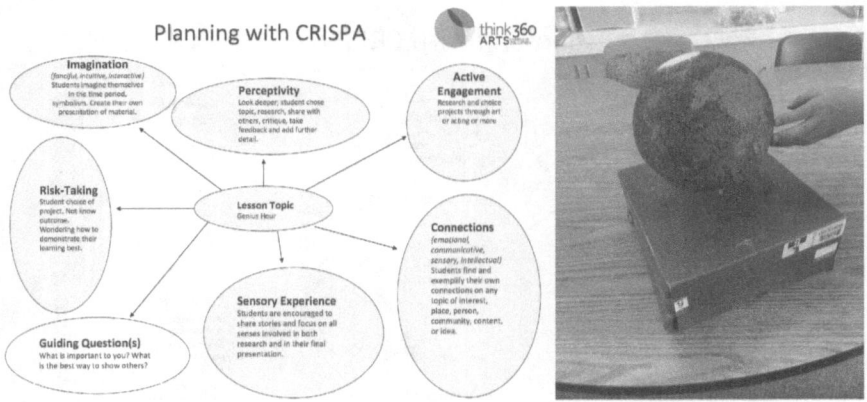

Figure 1.2. Example of fourth-grade genius hour CRISPA graphic organizer and one student's project. *Photo by Donna Goodwin.*

The students also kept individualized vocabulary journals, and when an unfamiliar word was introduced, students were encouraged to get their journals and create a vocabulary map by writing the word and definition, using it in a sentence, finding a synonym, and then drawing an illustration of the word and how it is used (see figure 1.3). These vocabulary words were discovered during all parts of the lesson including guest presentations, such as when a parent brought in a piñata and students experienced the fun of trying to break it open and enjoy the treats inside. The final assessment of the lesson in community traditions was a collaborative project where students worked together to create a collage of images along with a writing piece that demonstrated their understanding of community.

Tips from the Teachers

Both Sharon and Jane-Ellen were happy with the results of the lesson and believe strongly in using elements of CRISPA along with SIOP components. They stated that the students were more engaged than before and showed greater empathy with each other. They correlate this to

- allowing students more time to talk;
- using a variety of images and visuals;
- highlighting personal connections;
- incorporating more integrated movement such as acting out celebrations and cultural events;
- bringing in guest speakers; and
- allowing students to partner and do more collaborative work.

The BEAR C.L.A.W.
5th Grade Home Learning Menu

Community Involvement: Outings, Service Projects, and Teamwork	1. Help someone in your community with a need they may have and describe or draw what you did in your sketchbook. 2. Go to a local museum or library and describe what you experienced there. 3. Go to a park you have not gone to yet with a family member and describe the things and people you experienced. 4. Other – your choice: _____.	
Living with the Arts: Arts, Crafts, Drama, Music Performances, and Dance	1. Share with a family member about a book you are reading or something fun you've learned in math, literacy, science, or social studies, and create a visual arts piece with them based on the information you told them. 2. With a family member, write a fun song/rap about something you learned in math, literacy, science, or social studies. Sing it with each other and share it in your sketchbook. 3. Act out a skit of your choice based on something you have recently learned. Act out your skit at home and at school. 4. Other – your choice: _____.	
Academic: Reading, Writing, Math, Games, and Activities	1. Study your math facts or practice math concepts you learned the previous week. Write them out in your sketchbook. 2. Read your AR book or some other text that interests you and writ/draw in your sketchbook the main ideas from the pages you read. 3. Go online and research further something that you learned about in math, literacy, science, or social studies. Write about what you learned or illustrate it in a visual art piece. 4. Other – your choice: _____.	
Wellness: Outdoor or Physical Activities	1. Play a physically active game with your family, either outside or inside. Share in your sketchbook what you did by either writing or drawing. 2. Eat healthier by trying out a new recipe or a new snack or meal that is better for you to eat. Share your experience in your sketchbook by writing about it or drawing a picture. 3. Other – your choice: _____.	

Time is a gift.
Learn everywhere and any time.

Figure 1.3. Example of fifth-grade homework menu and one student's project.
Photo by Donna Goodwin.

One thing they plan to do differently next time is to incorporate more photography and allow students to take photos of family celebrations or bring in photos from home to add to the opening discussion and to the final collages rather than solely relying on images from Internet searches and magazines.

Fourth-Grade Stories

Kathleen Preston teaches fourth grade at Sherman Elementary and wanted to plan a yearlong unit using elements of CRISPA. She decided to model risk-taking for her students by introducing a new idea of a "genius hour" that will take place on Friday afternoons throughout the year. She introduced the idea and then let the students research and respond with a final project and presentation that can take any form they would like.

Description of the Lesson

Kathleen began the first "genius hour" by working through a brainstorming activity with the students to help them determine their passions and interests. She had them create a list of possible topics and ideas to explore and then to create their own guiding inquiry questions for the duration of the project. Through this activity she was fostering an environment of active engagement among the students. The topics students settled on were varied. Some examples are how to be a good manager of other people, determining why cats land on their feet, listing the most important events in their town throughout history, finding the best way to prevent injuries in football, and exploring dance customs around the world. In regard to this last topic, the student researched several countries and decided on a representative dance from each and then wrote a brief essay about these representative dances. For her final project and presentation she is in process of creating a globe on which she will eventually attach models of the dancers in matching attire attributed to the culture extending from the globe along with the country's flag.

Students do research on Friday afternoons using computers, the school library, and resources brought from home. Kathleen says that in the past students would very rarely remember to bring things back to school once they had taken them home; however, students are so engaged with their genius project that it has not been an issue this year. She notes how the students are doing creative and varied explorations. She has noticed their vocabulary broadening as they are learning new ideas, and she has begun encouraging them to keep a list of new vocabulary as evidence of their learning. At the time of this writing the projects are still ongoing, so there are no final results to share, but Kathleen is encouraged by what she describes as her students' deep thinking and passionate engagement in their genius work.

Tips from the Teacher

Kathleen reiterates frequently how she wishes there were more time to work on students' genius projects than just the one hour per week. She says that even now that hour can be encroached upon with other school requirements. She knew that doing the genius hour in the manner described in this paper would be an example of her own risk-taking, and she was open to allowing the genius time to develop as an organic process. However, Kathleen encourages other teachers to set a time limit for research and deadlines for certain parts of the project. She wishes she had helped students narrow their focus on topics sooner than she did. She warns that the class should have consistent access to technology and reliable Internet access for research. Students waiting on access to resources has been the only time when there have been behavioral issues during genius time.

While there are myriad ways the teachers at Sherman have incorporated elements of CRISPA to their sheltered language protocols, these two classroom lesson examples provide a glimpse of successful attempts to benefit student engagement and agency while still acquiring new content.

HOMEWORK MENUS

After seeing students become more engaged and involved in their learning in the classroom after incorporating CRISPA, the teachers decided to see if it could help them with another issue that had become difficult—homework. Teachers were hearing that parents and students felt overwhelmed with homework and it was a struggle to get students to finish all they had been assigned. Some parents felt too much time was spent on homework when they wanted to spend family time together. Other parents, in particular those learning a second language, described wanting to help their students but felt they did not always know how.

School staff decided to alter the way they think about homework and to use connections, risk-taking, imagination, sensory experience, perceptivity, and active engagement to link learning at school to experiences at home. Grade-level teacher teams created a homework menu: a list of options from which students and their families could choose from a variety of activities planned around the acronym CLAW. CLAW is a play on the school's mascot, the Bears, where C stands for community and family involvement, L is for living with the arts, A is for academics, and W stands for wellness.

Elements of CRISPA were present in the homework switch in several ways. First, by having students work with parents on homework, they were socially engaged and thus social connections were enacted (Moroye & Uhrmacher, 2012). Second, teachers, students, and parents were risk-taking by experimenting in ways that link school and home learning. There were fears that some might lose skills (e.g., math skills) or that it would be too fun and not enough learning would be involved. Imagination was present as students and parents had to decide how to link classroom learning through an activity on the CLAW menu and then when they created their own options for homework. Sensory experiences were encouraged in the CLAW throughout, but particularly in the wellness category when they explored healthy eating and exercising outdoors. Perceptivity is also encouraged throughout as students and parents are encouraged to pay close attention to where academic content is present in ordinary activities and to report back what they found. Finally, the entire purpose of the homework switch to the CLAW menu was to develop more active engagement and for students to take charge of their own home-to-school learning and sharing.

Second- and Third-Grade Stories

Second- and third-grade teachers decided to plan their homework menus together so that experiences in second grade would be recognized the following year and would therefore allow students to build on familiar territory. They received positive feedback from parents who appreciated being able to participate as a family in activities with their students as a part of homework. Both students and parents were able to create connections, an element of CRISPA. Several parents described how homework went from a frustrating and tearful event to something they could look forward to doing. One mother of an ELL student described how she felt her child was teaching her what he was learning in school and she felt more involved.

However, some parents feared their students were not being academically challenged when they could choose to play a game for homework instead of practicing a skill. One parent believed that options on the menu such as "having dinner together" felt judgmental as if the school were telling her how to parent. In addition, teachers struggled with wanting to require outside reading as additional homework, fearing students would not be reading enough if they chose to do other things. There is no long-term data at this point to determine an academic benefit or deficit from changing the homework requirements. However, there are several indicators that suggest it is not as much a struggle for parents as it was before and that all parents and students, including English learners, were more actively involved and were able to create connections with homework to their family and to their home life as well as school.

Fifth-Grade Stories

Fifth-grade teachers saw both successes and challenges with the homework menu. Some students were eager to take charge of their learning. For example, one student decided to research further the era they were studying in social studies, exemplifying communicative imagination. She drew and then created costumes for fictional characters, displaying the CRISPA elements of perceptivity, sensory experiences, and active engagement. She was able to link her learning to reading she was doing in her language arts class as well. Yet, other students struggled with deciding what to do when there were so many options. Some did not turn in work at all, feeling that since it was fun and not directly linked to a grade, it must be optional.

Fifth-grade teachers received feedback from some parents that they preferred traditional homework where students practiced skills such as mathematics, and they felt that by not being required to practice math problems, students would not do it on their own. Still other parents appreciated having the choice to decide on homework with their children and believed they learned more about what was going on in school by doing homework in this way. The CLAW menu is still an iterative process for fifth-grade teachers. They are experimenting with ways to make it work best for their students but do believe in the power of choice that active engagement provides. They are working now on ways in which students can more directly link the content they are learning in the classroom to the CLAW menu choices and perhaps be graded.

SUGGESTIONS AND RECOMMENDATIONS FOR THE K–12 PRACTITIONER

The staff of Sherman Elementary believes adding elements of CRISPA to their daily lessons and to their homework has been a success overall. They have noticed students are more engaged in their learning and are making choices about how to demonstrate what they know and are able to do. English language learners in particular have become more engaged as they have been able to bring in areas of their own understanding and culture, and they practice linguistic skills with their peers more than before. Despite the success, there have been hurdles. They provide the following suggestions for other teachers who would like to do something similar in their own schools and classrooms:

- Have a conversation with parents at the beginning of the year and determine a school-wide definition of the purpose of homework. Is it a home-to-school connection, a way to practice a skill, an enrichment activity, or something else? Provide translators and translations of all materials as necessary.

- Model and describe to students how the activities they are doing in class demonstrate and link to learning so they can eventually do so on their own.
- Develop a school-wide system of how homework is turned in or otherwise shared so it becomes a routine expectation.
- Allow students frequent choices during the school day so it becomes more natural. Teachers found students were so used to being told what to do that they were not easily able to make choices.
- Consciously create lessons using multiple modalities as examples for students to be able to demonstrate their learning in various ways.
- Give a choice of traditional homework along with the options listed on the menu.
- Plan all lessons, even those prescribed by a curriculum scope and sequence, around the elements of CRISPA, and denote where sheltered language instruction overlaps—try to do this more often.
- Don't talk too much—structure the day less on lecture and more on student grouping strategies where they can talk and research together and share what they have learned.

Resources

More information on CRISPA and perceptual teaching and learning can be found at http://www.crispateaching.org, along with example lesson plans and ways to incorporate CRISPA into various content areas. More information about creating a "genius hour" in the classroom can be found at https://www.teacherspayteachers.com.

Conclusion

There is not one way alone to meet the needs of all learners. The educational models mentioned above as well as myriad more that were not covered have the possibility to help children learn. Adding elements of CRISPA to classroom frameworks and instruction can open up the possibility for connection and engagement that might not otherwise be present in the day to day, especially among English language and other diverse learners.

NOTE

1. All names used for the school and teachers are pseudonyms.

REFERENCES

Applebee, A. N., Langer, J. A., Nystrand, M., & Gamoran, A. (2003). Discussion-based approaches to developing understanding: Classroom instruction and student performance in middle and high school English. *American Educational Research Journal, 40*, 685–730.

Arreaga-Mayer, C., & Perdomo-Rivera, C. (1996). Ecobehavioral analysis of instruction for at-risk language-minority students. *Elementary School Journal, 96*, 245–258.

Dewey, J. (1934). *Art as experience*. New York: Minton, Balch.

Echevarría, J., Vogt, M., & Short, D. J. (2012). *Making content comprehensible for English learners: The SIOP model*. 4th ed. Boston: Pearson.

Gardner, H. (2006). *Multiple intelligences: New horizons*. Rev. and updated. New York: Basic.

Gibbons, P. (2009). *English learners, academic literacy, and thinking: Learning in the challenge zone*. Portsmouth, NH: Heinemann.

Moroye, C. M., & Uhrmacher, P. B. (2009). Aesthetic themes of education. *Curriculum and Teaching Dialogue, 11*(1/2), 85–101.

Moroye, C. M., & Uhrmacher, P. B. (2010). Aesthetic themes as conduits to creativity. In C. J. Craig & L. F. Deretchin (Eds.), *Cultivating curious and creative minds: The role of teachers and teacher educators* (pp. 99–114). Lanham, MD: Rowman & Littlefield Education.

Moroye, C. M., & Uhrmacher, P. B. (2012). Standards, not standardization: Orchestrating aesthetic educational experiences. *Language Arts Journal of Michigan, 28*(13), 64–69.

National Center for English Language Acquisition (NCELA). (2015). English learner toolkit. Retrieved September 9, 2016, from http://www2.ed.gov/.

Peregoy, S., & Boyle, O. (2008). *Reading, writing and learning in ESL: A resource book for teaching K12 English learners*. Boston: Pearson.

Sousa, D. A. *How the brain learns*. 4th ed. Thousand Oaks, CA: Corwin, 2011.

Uhrmacher, P. B. (2009). Toward a theory of aesthetic learning experiences. *Curriculum Inquiry, 39*, 613–636.

Uhrmacher, P. B., & Bunn, K. E. (Eds.). (2011). *Beyond the one room school*. Rotterdam, Netherlands: SensePublishers.

Chapter Two

Sensemaking through Art Making

Trash for Teaching and Visual Arts Integration with Elementary Emergent Bilingual Students

Kristin Papoi

Third graders in small groups negotiate which materials from the classroom art center best illustrate the spikes of a cactus, the dryness of the desert floor, or the roughness of the sand. Productive talk between students abounds while small jars of green plastic widgets and shiny screws, bowls of commercially shredded paper, and boxes of colored pencils and oil pastels are scattered across tables. Teachers and arts pedagogists engage in purposeful questioning and formative assessment while students collaborate to use these materials to depict the living and nonliving elements of a desert habitat, replete with dimensional detail.

This scene happens daily in every classroom at Esperanza Charter Elementary School[1] in downtown Los Angeles; the school serves approximately 400 students, 99 percent of whom are Latino; 98 percent, socioeconomically disadvantaged; and 83 percent, English language learners, referred to in this chapter as emergent bilingual students (García, 2009). The work is facilitated using myriad interesting and repurposed materials provided by Trash for Teaching (T4T),[2] an organization that diverts safe and clean but discarded manufacturing by-products and overruns from landfills to classrooms across Southern California.

T4T materials serve as a scaffold to students, helping them to illustrate concepts they are learning while adults in the classroom are in constant dialogue with students to scaffold language and vocabulary using the materials and arts integration strategies. But the role of arts integration at Esperanza stretches beyond scaffolding and into sensemaking through the students' purposeful and thoughtful use of materials under the guidance of classroom teachers and the school's arts pedagogist.

Arts integration at Esperanza is inspired by the Reggio Emilia approach (Edwards, Gandini, & Forman, 1998), which views the child as capable and communicative, and is rooted in multiliteracy theory (Cope & Kalantzis, 2009; New London Group, 1996). Both approaches acknowledge that emergent bilingual students bring diverse resources to school that inform their learning through the influence of students' culture, communities, families, and linguistic backgrounds.

This chapter provides robust examples and evidence of how sensemaking through arts integration happens pedagogically using T4T materials. First, the arts integration cycle is explained along with the pedagogical structure and classroom design at Esperanza; then the affordances are detailed through examples of students in action. The chapter concludes with implications and resources for classroom practitioners who wish to engage in similar work in their own contexts.

THE ARTS INTEGRATION CYCLE AT ESPERANZA

Esperanza was "founded on the belief that every child has the potential to reach high standards of achievement, to ask good questions and to think critically" (charter organization website). The assistant principal, Ms. Solano, describes the purpose of the Reggio-inspired arts integration as deeply rooted in a project-based, constructivist approach. She explains how project-based work in the arts gives students time to dialogue and construct their own meaning by "have[ing] a voice in their learning, and when you actually give children that power, they take it and they actually do drive your lessons."

Facilitating this project-based arts integration work is the design of each classroom, each of which is arranged and designed in a Reggio Emilia aesthetic, with comfortable seating, natural light, and use of natural and home-based materials. Of note is the use of the student-accessible project center, called an *atelier* in the Reggio tradition, which is full of T4T materials that teachers have collected at the T4T warehouse (see figure 2.1) and space wherein students can work with these materials.

Teachers make solo and group trips to the warehouse throughout the year to collect materials for their ateliers—collecting items with certain learning units in mind (e.g., blue and red materials for a study of the human body with thoughts of how students can make sense of the paths of oxygenated and nonoxygenated blood in the body) or with the goal of finding interesting and novel materials for open-ended student exploration.

Following a Reggio Emilia framework, the project-based work at Esperanza integrates art making mostly into the science and social studies units of

Sensemaking through Art Making 19

Figure 2.1. Details of Esperanza classroom ateliers using curated T4T materials as provocations for student work on projects for a first-grade sound unit (top left) and a fourth-grade study of cells and organelles (bottom left). *Photos by Kristin Papoi.*

learning, aligned with the recently adopted Next Generation Science Standards (NGSS) and the College, Career, and Civic Life (C3) Social Studies Framework. Throughout each unit of study, students make meaning of their learning, starting with drawings of concepts in hardbound artist's sketchbooks. As Ms. Solano described the vital role of the sketchbooks, "[They] tell you a lot about the child, their experiences, and then they reflect on it too. And they know it's theirs, it's their sketchbook."

Sketches serve as the foundation for both student and teacher assessment of learning—the students show what they know visually, adding and changing items as they grow in their learning. Meanwhile, teachers use the sketches as formative assessments to understand student background knowledge or misconceptions. These sketchbooks follow students from kindergarten through their elementary experience and serve as a valuable portfolio documentation of their learning and thinking over time.

In addition to the sketching, students also work in small groups to explore different "provocations" such as books, videos, photographs, and realia related to the unit of study. Provocations, in the Reggio Emilia tradition, capture students' imagination through hands-on experience and allow for multiple ways of accessing, acquiring, and expressing knowledge, and group work around provocations provides students with firsthand experience of concepts and helps to tap into and build upon prior knowledge. Esperanza's school-wide arts pedagogist stressed the importance of providing firsthand experiences because "using the senses is so important, [making] learning academic language much easier than if you were reading, 'These are the states of matter, and this is a solid.' But if you're touching it and feeling it, then learning the language becomes much easier."

In addition to these small-group provocations, each classroom also has an ongoing, Reggio Emilia–inspired, documentation display—a learning wall where student work in progress is presented in a way that honors the processes, words, and multiple languages of children's expression. The documentation display contains unit resources including keyword vocabulary, unit learning goals and standards, teacher-student created charts, and student sensemaking work such as drawings and models. The wall evolves over the course of the unit as students add new work, provocations, and class charts containing the students' words and ideas.

Finally, at the end of the school year, each classroom—in conjunction with the students, teacher, arts pedagogist, and the artist-in-residence—decides upon a final culminating project for Art Week. Art Week is an annual event where students synthesize their learning through the creation of collaborative art pieces, which both display what they have learned and apply that to the creation of new knowledge.

This culminating celebration is also rooted in the Reggio Emilia tradition, which invites the community to take part in the expression of learning. The ongoing cycle of arts integration at Esperanza from individual 2-D/3-D representation to small-group work and whole-class collaborative work repeats itself in each unit of study and culminates in the final Art Week exhibition, where students invite their families to view and discuss the final pieces. While the culminating projects are compellingly beautiful and ingenious, the process behind these projects is where the real learning takes place for the students.

IMPLEMENTING A PEDAGOGY OF PARTICIPATION

The arts integration approach taken up at Esperanza using the T4T materials creates a unique space for emergent bilingual student learning that is facilitated by a *pedagogy of participation*. Specifically, a pedagogy of participation provides a context in which students can participate in ways that are relevant and meaningful to them because it incorporates what we know about what works for emergent bilingual students, including productive group work; opportunities for oral language development; additional supports within proven instructional strategies; explicit vocabulary instruction; and connecting to students' linguistic and cultural assets (August & Shanahan, 2006; Gibbons, 2015; Goldenberg, 2013).

The pedagogy of participation facilitates multiple opportunities and ways for students to legitimately engage in a variety of linguistic and nonlinguistic modes because the pedagogy itself brings forth multiple valid methods of participation. The following components essential to the pedagogy of participation are illustrated through classroom examples at Esperanza, which can be reproduced in other classroom contexts. First, group work is a core and central part to what happens at Esperanza. Second, the pedagogy facilitates sensemaking through the creation of both 2-D and 3-D art using T4T materials that serve as both a form of meaning making as well as a form of assessment.

The affordances of arts integration work at Esperanza through the pedagogy of participation are described for the remainder of this chapter and can be applied to a variety of school contexts.

LEARNING THE POWER OF WORKING IN A GROUP

Productive group work is an integral component for emergent bilingual student learning within a pedagogy of participation where talk is necessary for the task, a clear goal is at hand, and the work is integrated into the larger curriculum (Gibbons, 2015). The group work is highly integrated into all parts of the day at Esperanza, almost without notice of its seamless integration, because it is such a regular part of the classroom routine. As one teacher explained, "It's just what we do."

Group work affords several pedagogical advantages that are important for emergent bilingual students, namely firsthand experiences, oral language opportunities, time for thinking and doing, and, finally, iterative group work. Each of these ideas is explored and illustrated by the following examples of arts-integration work from Esperanza.

Language Development through Firsthand Experiences

At the beginning of any learning unit at Esperanza—and throughout—the students typically engage with groups to explore firsthand experiences. Their purpose is to provide multimodal opportunities for students to engage with experience, which is more meaningful than simply hearing a teacher talk about a concept or the students reading the information in a book. The T4T materials provided in the atelier are the focal point of these experiences because the materials therein facilitate opportunities for oral language development.

Language scaffolding takes place as students explore materials, experiment to construct something, and explain what they made to peers and teachers. For example, the T4T materials are so varied and unique—buttons, metal fixtures, plastic tubes, zippers, and so forth—that students naturally engage in rich vocabulary usage as they explore the materials to problem solve and find just the right thing for what they are representing (such as in the desert example at the beginning of this chapter where a student used pointy plastic objects that he felt would best represent the "sharpness" and "spikes" on the cactus).

Ms. Solano summed up the power of the group to facilitate language production:

> A lot of the students are hesitant to speak because of the language, they might not know the right word, so offering children opportunities to practice and use language is important. [That's why] it's important for students to learn the power of being able to work in a group, and so, having those conversations about negotiating, and again, allowing children the opportunity to speak in the class and problem solve, is a very important part of this process, especially for language learners.

Iterative Group Work

Aligned with the affordances to produce oral language within the group work setting is the idea of *iterative group work*, where groups expand and contract in size and purpose, much like an accordion. An example of how this works at Esperanza begins with a whole-group discussion with the teacher around an artifact or experience (e.g., watching a YouTube video about sound waves or during a whole-class read-aloud). Then, students break into small groups to engage with planned, intentional experiences, through which students circulate throughout the day or week, depending on the length of the unit.

After small-group work, the whole group reconvenes to make sense of what was learned; then they break apart again into different small groups to engage with other new experiences. This is facilitated by discussion between students and with adults in the room that incorporate questioning and vocabulary scaffolding. The key idea in iterative group work is that sometimes the work is individual, and sometimes it is collective.

In one first-grade class's work on a science unit about sound, small groups worked together to explore instruments and then to create sound stories through sketches. Then, they reconvened class to take a neighborhood "sound walk." After debriefing the walk, they split up to create individual drawings that illustrated how they understood that sound traveled in waves in all directions.

Students based their drawings upon the experiences they had in small and large groups together, using pictures of sound waves as their guide. Toward the end of the unit the students worked in small groups on a class mural depicting their notions of sound traveling in all directions. They also used the T4T materials to build a working wind chime that could create beautiful sounds. Figure 2.2 presents a sequence of artifacts illustrating iterative group work in this first-grade sound unit, illustrating student learning within the science content standards about the properties of sounds (e.g., sound moves in waves in all directions).

SENSEMAKING AS FORM OF ASSESSMENT: "THEY SAW THEMSELVES AS RESEARCHERS"

In addition to the affordances of T4T arts-based practices to facilitate meaningful group work, they also provide a valuable language to emergent bilingual students and their teachers for both sensemaking and assessment. Sensemaking generally refers to the ways that people make meaning from an

Figure 2.2. Progression of first-grade students' work in the sound unit. (*Left to right*) Individual student sketches of triangle and maracas showing sound waves moving in all directions and using onomatopoeia, collective 2-D class representation of sound painted on canvas that include elements from the sketches, and 3-D representation of a wind chime created by multiple students using T4T materials. *Left and middle photos by Kristin Papoi; right photo by classroom teacher.*

experience; in this case, it means learning through arts integration experiences.

At Esperanza, sensemaking through art-based practices is a highly valuable assessment, but there is often a project-writing component where students write about what they did and what they understood—a more traditional literary expression. Ms. Solano said that by moving through a 2-D (sketches) to 3-D (T4T materials) process, "the students saw themselves as researchers" who have "lots of questions and felt very comfortable asking questions and participating in discussions." Sensemaking as a form of assessment relies on questioning to uncover misconceptions, along with the engineering of a final project, as described in the examples below.

Questioning as Assessment

Asking questions is essential to the arts integration process at Esperanza, whether it is students or teachers asking the questions. A powerful example of this happened in the second-grade class's exploration of the desert habitat. Students were working on depicting 2-D desert habitat scenes, paying close attention to the interaction between living and nonliving things. A boy and a girl were taking inspiration from a book photograph of a very dry and cracked desert landscape and were tearing sand-colored paper into shapes that they placed on their paper to capture the look of the terrain.

Upon seeing the students' work and after establishing that the desert floor was a nonliving thing, the arts pedagogist and the researcher engaged them in the following discussion on the interdependence of living and nonliving things in the desert:

> Linda (arts pedagogist): I mean, the thing is, not a lot of living things could really live in this because why?
>
> Boy: There's no water and there's no food.
>
> Linda: There's very, very little water and food; you're absolutely right. So maybe in this picture it doesn't look like much is living, does it?
>
> Girl: No.
>
> Researcher: I was wondering if animals like to be in the shade of the little cracks.
>
> Linda [to students]: Yeah, I think that's a really good question, actually, if there is anything living in between these cracks. What do you think? If there was anything that might live in there, what might live in there?

Girl: A lizard!

Linda: But what would they live on? Remember, they need water and food. I don't know if there's anything in there.

Boy: Maybe on the top it's dry but on the bottom there is water.

Linda: That's a really great point, so there might be something inside there. Maybe there is some water underneath. Can I ask you guys to think about that as a question? What question can we ask? How can you turn that into a question so we can talk about that at the end of all this? What question would you ask about this?

Boy: How cracks are made in the desert?

Linda: Well, what do we want to know? Are there any living things in the cracks? Can anything live here, right?

Girl: Oh! How animals can live here?

After this exchange, the two students scoured the book resources to find evidence of insects or small lizards living under the cracked desert floor. Linda summarized the dynamism of students asking questions through working collaboratively in groups on arts integration projects:

> Children feel confident to take risks, to ask questions, to make mistakes, and that is a very unusual thing. You could tell even though some children struggle to put the sentence together . . . [but] they felt okay to ask a question. To ask a lot of questions. And good questions, and rich questions, and not just simple questions that require yes or no, but they were deep questions.

Uncovering Student Misconceptions

Sensemaking through art-making at Esperanza also helps teachers and the arts pedagogist to identify student misconceptions. By using 2-D pictures and 3-D models created around their learning, students are presented with opportunities to talk about their knowledge within the context of the artifact. Additionally, the act of talking during the art-making process uncovers misconceptions.

One example of this emerged during another second-grade class's exploration of pollinators. Students had been working on their habitat exploration and were concerned about the ramifications of the extinction of bees. "How will we help the bees?" they began to ask, so one group of students created a "pollinator machine" from T4T materials such as cardboard tubes, rings, flat cardboard cut into a circle, wire, and pushpins. The ingenious contraption pivoted on an axis so the wire could move from one set of flowers to another, acting as a pollinator (see figure 2.3).

During the explanation of how the machine worked, the following conversation transpired:

> Student: We're trying to see which one [flower] does better. This one is almost dead and that one is almost dead, but these are not dead because . . .
>
> KP: Because it's closer?
>
> Student: Yes, it's getting pollinated.
>
> KP: So if they don't get pollen do they die?
>
> Student: Yes, and if there's no more pollinators, there's no more food, and we die. And nothing else survives.

Questioning through the artifact revealed the student's misconception that pollination helps to keep flowers alive, when in reality lack of pollination prevents flowers from reproducing and therefore less flowers will be pro-

Figure 2.3. The pollinator machine that helped the teacher and teaching artists uncover student misconceptions about the process of pollination. *Photos by Kristin Papoi.*

duced. The student did understand the magnitude of importance of the pollinators but had some of the smaller details incorrect. Using the model to talk through the pollination process helped uncover and correct the misconception.

IMPLICATIONS/RECOMMENDATIONS

The following implications and recommendations resulting from the study of T4T at Esperanza revolve around the essential question *What does this mean for emergent bilingual student learning?* The ideas are intentionally presented as questions rather than statements because every educational context is unique with different goals, restraints, and student needs.

The most important consideration for classroom teachers from this case study that will directly impact student and teacher experience is the idea of pedagogy of participation and the surrounding concepts of iterative group work, opportunities for oral language afforded by the arts, and the role the visual arts play in sensemaking for meaning and assessment. Questions for practicing teachers include the following:

- What arts modalities are comfortable for me to bring into my classroom?
- What resources can help me to facilitate learning through the arts? (For example, see Topal & Gandini, 1999.)
- Where can I implement multimodal expression into existing curriculum to deepen and expand student learning?
- How can I use the arts as a tool for "knowing" rather than "showing" for my culturally and linguistically diverse students? How can I integrate the arts across my curriculum to build meaning about content (e.g., showing interactions or critical thinking) rather than treat it as a decoration or "add-on"?
- How can I use questioning and group work in the visual arts to assess my students' knowledge to meet their needs through reteaching and future lessons? (See Gibbons, 2015, as a resource for questioning and productive group work.)
- How can I arrange my classroom space to allow for iterative group work? An atelier? Staging of content-rich provocations? An interactive documentation wall?
- What local, state, and national grants are available that would support visual arts-based programs at my school? What resources can I tap into to apply for them?
- Where can I resource materials for a classroom atelier? Are there local organizations I could contact (similar to T4T) or manufacturers that would

donate materials I could repurpose in my classroom for arts-based learning?

Classroom teachers are so often called upon to go "above and beyond" that these recommendations, on first glance, seem to fall heavily upon their shoulders. However, with support from district and school administrators they are valid and attainable.

In summary, there are wide-ranging implications for PK–12 educators that emerge from this study that warrant investigation in relation to the educators' specific context. By asking the questions posed above, in addition to creating their own questions in specific relation to their educational context, educators can successfully be inspired to implement the powerful pedagogy of participation to positively impact emergent bilingual student learning and classroom experiences.

NOTES

1. Pseudonyms are used for the school, charter organization, teachers, and students in this chapter.
2. For more information about the Trash for Teaching organization, see http://www.t4t.org.

REFERENCES

August, D., & Shanahan, T. (Eds.). (2006). *Developing literacy in second-language learners: Report of the National Literacy Panel on Language-Minority Children and Youth.* Mahwah, NJ: Erlbaum.

Cope, B., & Kalantzis, M. (2009). Multiliteracies: New literacies, new learning. *Pedagogies: An International Journal, 4,* 164–195.

Edwards, C., Gandini, L., & Forman, G. (1998). *The hundred languages of children: The Reggio Emilia approach; Advanced reflections.* 2nd ed. Westport, CT: Ablex.

García, O. (2009). Emergent bilinguals and TESOL: What's in a name? *TESOL Quarterly, 43*(2), 322–326.

Gibbons, P. (2015). *Scaffolding language, scaffolding learning: Teaching English language learners in the mainstream classroom.* Portsmouth, NH: Heinemann.

Goldenberg, C. (2013). Unlocking the research on English learners: What we know—and don't yet know—about effective instruction. *American Educator, 37*(2), 4.

New London Group. (1996). A pedagogy of multiliteracies: Designing social futures. *Harvard Educational Review, 66*(1), 60–92.

Topal, C. W., & Gandini, L. (1999). *Beautiful stuff! Learning with found materials.* Worcester, MA: Davis.

Chapter Three

Photo Elicitation

Using Photography with Elementary ELL Students

Carissa Natalewicz

Photo elicitation is the practice of using photographs and other visual images to gather responses from those who are viewing them (Hatten, Forin, & Adams, 2013). Research supports that using photo elicitation helps increase memory and expand on knowledge, while also decreasing potential misunderstandings about topics (Harper, 2002). Using photography in education is a very beneficial tool that can be implemented in all grade levels.

This method is particularly helpful when children have verbal limitations or when language barriers exist (Jenkings, Woodward, & Winter, 2008). In a 2012 study by Kristien Zenkov and colleagues, English language learner (ELL) middle school students were asked to use photographs to describe their feelings about school. The researchers found that when analyzing the photographs solely independently, the students had difficulty coming up with ideas to write. However, when done first as a whole group, then in small groups, and then independently, the students were more eager and motivated to begin writing.

To feel comfortable and become successful as they grow, English language learners must frequently interact with their peers and be given opportunities to openly participate in class discussions (Mohr & Mohr, 2007). Discussing various photographs in whole-group settings can be beneficial to these students in particular because it takes pressure off of them getting a "right" or "wrong" answer. Since each interpretation is unique to the person who is sharing it, ELL students can actively participate without feeling any embarrassment over voicing their thoughts and ideas (Moran & Tegano, 2005).

USING PHOTOGRAPHY IN EDUCATION

Teachers can use photography to enhance daily lessons and to promote constructive communication between students and their peers. Four specific examples will be shared that have been used successfully in lower elementary classrooms:

1. A science lesson on seasons
2. Daily fun facts
3. Close observations of photos
4. Using photos for writing prompts

Each of the mentioned strategies resulted in positive outcomes for all students, including English language learners who were present in the classrooms.

Seasons Lesson

When classes start a unit on seasons, each student should keep a journal to document his or her explorations. A great, visual way to teach the changes that occur during different seasons is to show students photographs to compare (see figures 3.1 and 3.2).

This strategy works best when all the photos are taken in the same spot. Depending on the grade level, teachers have flexibility in how they implement this lesson. It can be an ongoing lesson throughout the year where the class goes outside to observe as the seasons change. When done this way, the teacher could take a photo each time and then the photos can be printed or displayed on a projector for the students to compare (once in the fall, once in the winter, once in the spring, and once in the summer).

Observing the photographs as a whole group and discussing them helps the students have meaningful conversations, develop strong questioning skills, and learn new vocabulary words. For example, students in the past have inquired as follows:

- Why does that tree have no leaves?
- Why does that tree's leaves have different colors?
- Why does the ground look different from one photo compared to the other?

These wonderings of natural phenomena can provide the teacher with opportunities to educate the students about photosynthesis that gives a plant food, chlorophyll that makes the leaves green, or a dormant tree "sleeping" in the winter that has bare branches.

Figure 3.1. March trees and stream, Lawrence, NJ. *Photo by Carissa Natalewicz, 2016.*

After the whole-group discussions, students can then work in small groups or independently to write in a "seasons journal." They can use what they know from their outdoor observations, from comparing the photos, and from listening to their peers to help them describe the different seasons. Though ELL students will still need extra support with the writing piece, having them actively observe and participate in discussions first will help prime their ideas and make this step a little easier for them.

With students who are a little older and have the available resources, it can be their job to take the photos each time the class goes out to observe the changing seasons. This would help them "own" the photos and would make the project unique and meaningful to them. They could share their photos with their peers and discuss the similarities and differences between them.

If teachers do not want to make this an ongoing project of field observations, it can still be implemented without that step. They can simply skip that part and instead just show students the two photos of different seasons to compare. When students are comparing and contrasting the photos out loud in a group discussion, this also provides the teacher with an opportunity to

Figure 3.2. October trees and stream, Lawrence, NJ. *Photo by Carissa Natalewicz, 2016.*

clear up any misconceptions that the children might have (for example, if they think it only rains during one season).

Daily Fun Facts

The next method takes a little more preparation to execute, but once it is done, it can be used year after year. Teachers show students a daily photograph called a "fun fact" and tell a surprising, strange, or interesting fact that goes along with it. This can be presented at any time but works especially well at the beginning of the day to get their minds thinking. It is something that students look forward to because it is typically something so bizarre that they cannot believe it is true. They will frequently go home and tell their families about the exciting fact that they learned for the day.

For example, try projecting an image of a dolphin jumping out of the water and then announce the following fun fact: dolphins are not fish. Next, explain that dolphins are mammals because they breathe air with lungs, have hair, and give birth to live young. The children should then be given time to observe the photograph and share some more facts, such as "the water is blue" and "the sun is shining."

After showing a fun fact, teachers can give students a few extra minutes to comment about it and ask questions aloud. A "wonder wall" can also be created, allowing students to use sticky notes to write down what they wonder about the fact. When implemented, fun facts are a great way to promote positive discussions and interactions between peers. Teachers can also scaffold good questioning by modeling "I wonder [how, why, if, when, where, or who]" statements for the students to use. For instance, after the dolphin example, some students might wonder if there are other mammals that live in water.

The fun facts can be about anything true, though most students get very excited any time a rare deep-sea creature is involved. They enjoy learning about different animals, things in space, and anything in the world that is the tallest, smallest, fastest, longest, and so forth. Teachers can add in facts about holidays or even award-winning LEGO®[1] towers that required the collaboration of hundreds of children. The possibilities are endless.

Since it can be intimidating to come up with a fact for every day, teachers can begin by showing one "weekly" fact that the students get to see every Monday or Friday. Throughout the school year, they can increase the frequency of the facts as they find them. Teachers can also collaborate with their grade-level educators to compile enough fun facts for the year. After that, the same facts can be used repeatedly with each new group of enthusiastic students.

Fun facts are a great way to bring in all subject areas and can also incorporate student interests. Teachers just starting with them can get input from the students, asking what they would like to know about the world and describing what research is. It could even be a project for older students to do their own research and find facts to share with the class. Anything that gets them wondering more about the world around them will have a positive impact on their learning.

Close Photo Observations

Another activity teachers can have students do is observe photos closely, which can be done in a variety of ways. One way to involve everyone is to show students a photograph with a lot of details and ask the students to each come up with a "wonder" or a "notice" about the photo. Before sharing aloud, the students can show a signal with their fingers once they have their idea. This is great for all students, including English language learners, because everyone could participate. It also takes pressure off the students who have trouble coming up with a wonder (or question) by allowing them to simply add in a comment about the photo.

Teachers can also show two unrelated photographs and ask the students to find something that is the same in them. Though there may be some visual details that are the same (colors, shapes, height, objects, etc.), this provides students with an opportunity to think "outside of the box." With a little practice, the students can make thoughtful connections between the photos they observe.

Since children love playing "I spy," teachers can create a similar game that will encourage all students to participate in observing photos closely. They can display a photo with various objects in it (similar to an "I spy" page) and let the students know they will have 30 seconds to look closely at it. After time is up, the photo is taken away and the students must try to recall as many objects as they can. This is a great activity to build language skills, while also enhancing memory and critical thinking in every student.

Nonfiction images of objects, scenes, or interesting people work great for close observations because they give students a chance to enhance their vocabulary and describe what is going on in the photos. The photos can open up discussions about synonyms and antonyms, which is particularly beneficial to students learning English. They can also demonstrate different points of view and allow students to think in diverse ways.

Writing Prompts

The final example is using photographs as prompts for verbal and written stories in a classroom. With this strategy, teachers of younger elementary students can first display a photograph and model both types of stories with the class. They can then perform a "shared writing" activity where they work together to develop characters, a setting, a problem, and a solution. The final goal is for the students to develop stories on their own based on the provided photographs.

Another way to execute this idea is to keep a basket of magazine photos, which teachers may laminate if they want to reuse them. When doing it this way, the students can create stories based on their chosen photo. Providing them with a choice of photos ensures they will pick something that interests them and sparks a story idea. During the writing phase, teachers can provide extra support to any ELL students who are having difficulty getting their stories onto paper.

This method is a great tool to help students think creatively and to plan their ideas. The photos also assist English language learners by providing them with a concrete visual aid and a straightforward starting point. After the students finish their stories, teachers can have them share their ideas in small groups. This presents all students with another opportunity to safely share their ideas aloud, helping them realize that everyone's ideas are unique and valuable.

BENEFITS OF USING PHOTOGRAPHY WITH ELL STUDENTS

Using photography in education benefits all students, though it is especially helpful for English language learners. Teachers notice that these students are much more eager to participate in lessons when photos are involved. Since they can interpret the photographs in their own way and do not have to focus only on reading or writing, it makes them feel more comfortable sharing their ideas with their peers. This helps build their confidence in language and takes away some of the barriers they often face when learning.

This method of teaching also builds positive peer relationships and teaches the students to be accepting of others' thoughts and opinions. As they share their ideas through meaningful discussions, the students listen to one another and construct new meanings of words and ideas. Students expand on their vocabulary knowledge and can think creatively without feeling embarrassed since there is no "right" or "wrong" answer.

Another positive result of using photographs in education is that it helps all students develop critical-thinking skills. When students view photographs of the world around them, they naturally develop questions, comments, and connections that relate to the pictures. With practice, they engage in productive conversations with one another and come up with deep, thoughtful questions about the topics.

TIPS

One essential tip when using photo elicitation in the classroom is to provide students with a sufficient amount of "think time." So often, teachers dislike the uncomfortable silence after asking a question and will choose the first student impulsively raising his or her hand to give an answer. To help foster the deep critical thinking that comes out of these activities, giving all students time to think is important.

Some teachers even like to eliminate hand-raising during such lessons and will instead have students hold up fingers close to their chest. If the students have one idea, they hold up one finger. If they have two ideas, they hold up two fingers, and so on. This method is much more private and eliminates students feeling pressure to have their hands up high in the air as soon as a question is asked. It also provides teachers with valuable insight, seeing who may have trouble coming up with an idea and will need a little assistance.

For photo elicitation to work best in a class, it is essential that teachers first foster a positive learning environment. The students need to know that their ideas are valued by both their teachers and their peers before feeling comfortable enough to share their thoughts freely out loud. The open-ended nature of these activities will spark a lot of creativity in suitable environments. Setting ground rules that the students must respect one another and that everyone's opinions matter will help it be successful.

When implementing these methods in a classroom, the types of photos chosen should be ones that are interesting to the students. At times, having photos that the students can easily relate to will help generate ideas, especially for ELL students. It is equally important to have some photographs that are more complex, perhaps something the students have never seen before. These kinds of photos will generate more thoughtful questions from the students and will simultaneously encourage critical thinking.

To do any of the activities mentioned in this chapter, teachers can use whichever resources they have available to them. Those who work in schools with updated technology may choose to show photos on a projector, Smart Board, or PowerPoint presentation. Others may want to use posters, printouts, or photos from magazines that they display on the white board (which they could choose to laminate if they want to keep for a longer time span).

Personal experiences, interests, and prior knowledge all affect the way people view photographs. When students share their varying opinions about photos aloud, new understandings and differing points of view can be observed (Moran & Tegano, 2005). The rich discussions that are created through photo elicitation help build vocabulary and also support inquiry-based teaching. Overall, it is an excellent tool that educators can use on a daily basis to support learning in all academic areas.

ADDITIONAL RESOURCES

One excellent website that teachers can use to find photographs is http://www.pics4learning.com. This site consists of safe and free photos that can be used in any classroom, either printed out or displayed on a screen. It has the photographs separated by genre: animals, countries, food, education, space, and geography. Once teachers choose the genre they want, other categories within each genre are displayed. This is a very valuable resource that is easily accessible and provides teachers with a variety of options.

Another beneficial photo website is http://www.akidsphoto.com. On the main page, teachers can choose from different categories: critter photos, floral photos, scenic photos, or object photos. Just like the previous website, these photos are free of charge and the site offers an assortment of kid-friendly photographs. Teachers can find some unique photo categories at http://www.copyrightfreephotos.com. This website has options such as "technology," "transport," and "buildings." These categories provide photographs with a lot of detail that would be great to use for close photo observations.

NOTE

1. LEGO® is a registered trademark of the LEGO group.

REFERENCES

Harper, D. (2002). Talking about pictures: A case for photo elicitation. *Visual Studies, 17*(1), 13–26. doi:10.1080/14725860220137345.
Hatten, K., Forin, T. R., & Adams, R. (2013). A picture elicits a thousand meanings: Photo elicitation as a method for investigating cross-disciplinary identity development. *American Society for Engineering Education*. https://www.asee.org/.
Jenkings, K. N., Woodward, R., & Winter, T. (2008). The emergent production of analysis in photo elicitation: Pictures of military identity. *Forum: Qualitative Sozialforschung/Forum: Qualitative Social Research, 9*(3). http://nbn-resolving.de/.
Mohr, K., & Mohr, E. (2007). Extending English language learners' classroom interactions using the response protocol. *Reading Teacher, 60*(5), 440–450. http://www.readingrockets.org/.
Moran, M. J., & Tegano, D. (2005). Moving toward visual literacy: Photography as a language of teacher inquiry. *Early Childhood Research and Practice, 7*(1). http://ecrp.uiuc.edu/.
Zenkov, K., Ewaida, M., Bell, A., & Lynch, M. (2012, November). Seeing how to ask first: Photo elicitation motivates English language learners to write. *Middle School Journal*, 6–13. http://files.eric.ed.gov/.

Chapter Four

Becoming a Community

How an Arts-Integrated Curriculum Supported the Development of English Language Learners in a Kindergarten Classroom

Rebecca Garte and Michelle Allen

In a Title I elementary school in Central Harlem, one teacher implemented an emergent, inquiry-based curriculum with a highly diverse group of kindergartners. Among these children, three entered the class in September speaking no English.

This chapter describes a variety of activities and experiences that unfolded from the needs and skills of the children. Emergent curriculum is teaching grown out of what the children show that they want to know and need to learn; it is teaching in response to what children are doing. The story of this kindergarten year is situated in the context of a real-life classroom to provide an example of how to develop activities and experiences that use art as a medium to support English language learners (ELLs).

INCLUSIVITY THROUGH ART

Art was an especially salient medium for one of these children, Amy, from the moment she entered the classroom. As recalled by her teacher, "Amy was quiet and solitary, an outlier and a mystery to many of her peers. She had been born in China, moved to India, and had recently arrived in the United States. Her mother told me that they spoke almost exclusively Chinese in their home where she was also cared for by her grandmother and father who spoke no English."

Over the course of the year, Amy and the other ELLs moved from the periphery of the kindergarten's community of learners to its center. Their social and linguistic development occurred within a sociocultural context (Rogoff, 2003). Art can also be useful in documenting how children change. Through children's art, teachers can see how to make learning meaningful, particularly for students who are less able to convey their ideas in English.

Art offers a universally accessible medium that enables an inclusive community to develop among a wide diversity of children. Art making and references to art products facilitate communication by providing a scaffold (Bruner, 1996) for children's language. The teacher profiled in this chapter created a variety of activities that integrated art and embedded standards while providing opportunities for authentic assessment of each child.

Rather than providing an activity to use art to support ELLs in the classroom, this chapter suggests an approach to children and to curriculum. At the center of this approach is a set of values that form the basis of the classroom community. Giving children ownership of the space of the classroom and a way to meaningfully navigate its many areas provided grounding during the initial transition to the class and through subsequent transitions. Using art to connect the children to the classroom space was particularly effective for ELLs. Allowing curriculum to emerge out of the natural inclinations and discoveries of the children also allowed the methods of curriculum, such as exploration and manipulation of materials, to emerge from the diverse interests and skills of the class, including the ELLs.

Finally, focusing on the connections between subjects supported each individual child's meaning-making experiences. For ELLs, an arts-integrated approach to curriculum provided an entry point for their participation. As the ELLs' degree of participation increased, their use of English language did as well. Consistent with a sociocultural view of development, meaningful participation in a community and language development are considered parallel processes. The methods detailed below supported each of these processes and led to increased English language proficiency and full class participation by the English language learners.

CREATING COMMUNITY THROUGH ARTS-BASED CONVERSATION

Each art activity is introduced and modeled as a mini lesson by the teacher in a whole-group setting (no more than five minutes) using new vocabulary. Children can choose the art activity during project time over the course of the week. Teachers record individual children's comments and descriptions and attach the dictations to their artwork. The final product is displayed in the classroom for all to see and reflect upon.

This process facilitates conversation and communication, initially as teachers help children figure out what they want to say about their work, and later as children describe their work to parents and peers. In this way, the art serves as a scaffold for communicating through conversation. From the introduction of art activities to the reflection on the final product, the art mediates children's ideas and understandings and supports their ability to express those ideas in English. The permanent installations of ongoing project work allow children to express themselves as unique individuals as well as members of a community of learners.

Whole-class experiences with concrete materials provide a shared reference point among the class that also allows equal access for ELLs. For example, outside exploration in a park yields collections of artifacts that are brought into the classroom to be observed closely, supporting children's awareness and descriptions of similarities and differences. These collective experiences that tie curriculum to found objects help develop a class identity and common interests.

ACTIVITIES USING ART TO SUPPORT ELLS IN KINDERGARTEN

Beginning Activities to Nurture a Sense of Belonging during September

- Pencil drawings. Place inside each cubby to signify personal space.
- Easel painting. Available during choice time; display in a classroom "gallery" above each child's full name to create a border along the entire perimeter of the classroom.
- Watercolor with felt-tip pens. Guided by the chant "Swish, swish, dab, dab, wiggle, wiggle, paint on paper." After painting the teacher provides children with a felt-tip black pen to draw on top of the dried paint. The teacher elicits children's observations about the differences between the two mediums and affixes a small, black-and-white photo of each child to the bottom of the work. A montage of all the watercolor/pen artwork is taped to the front door of the classroom.

These open-ended activities provide a concrete means of connecting the children, including the ELLs, to the classroom space. Any one of these activities could serve a similar purpose for teachers looking to help smooth the beginning-of-the-year transition for young children.

Art Embedded in an Emergent Curriculum

- Monthly self-portraits. Children sit in pairs opposite each other facing a double-sided mirror. The teacher introduces the activity with a series of read-alouds that discusses facial features, similar and different, and the process of making a portrait such as "reflection" and "detail." The books can include the following: *We Are All Alike . . . We Are All Different (Todos somos iguales . . . Todos somos diferentes)*, *What I Like about Me!*, *The Colors of Us*, and *Same, Same but Different*.

Self-portraits have long been used as an authentic assessment tool. As children develop, their portraits become increasingly accurate and detailed. In addition to documenting children's cognitive development, the teacher used self-portraits to introduce the concepts of similarities and differences and to teach about human diversity, a major social studies concept in kindergarten.

This activity paired visual representations with concepts and vocabulary, which supported the comprehension of the ELLs. The ELLs can make connections between the way their partner describes facial details and what they see in their own mirror. In addition, the entire activity allows for repetition of the same vocabulary in slightly varied contexts, an ideal situation for language learning (Cazden, 2001).

- Materials study. The class delves into an investigation of material properties and their relationship to art-making processes. Materials such as paper are broken down and re-created, then used in art and scientific experiments.
- Using found objects to focus curriculum. Children collect natural objects from the park each day and bring them into the classroom. The teacher places these objects in all the learning centers to focus children's observations, investigations, and conversations.
- "Messing about" table for sensory exploration, of first sand then soil.

The hands-on explorations with shared materials allowed the ELL children to relate new words to actions and objects. In addition, listening to conversations about similar objects in many ways throughout the classroom and describing their properties repeatedly while observing English-dominant peers discuss the same observations and ideas promoted English language learning. These hands-on experiences connected the ELLs to the classroom curriculum and shared focus of study. Figure 4.1 presents the many ways these objects can be available within learning centers.

- Tree study that emerged from ongoing hands-on exploration. By tying the first thematic unit of study to children's everyday shared experiences with

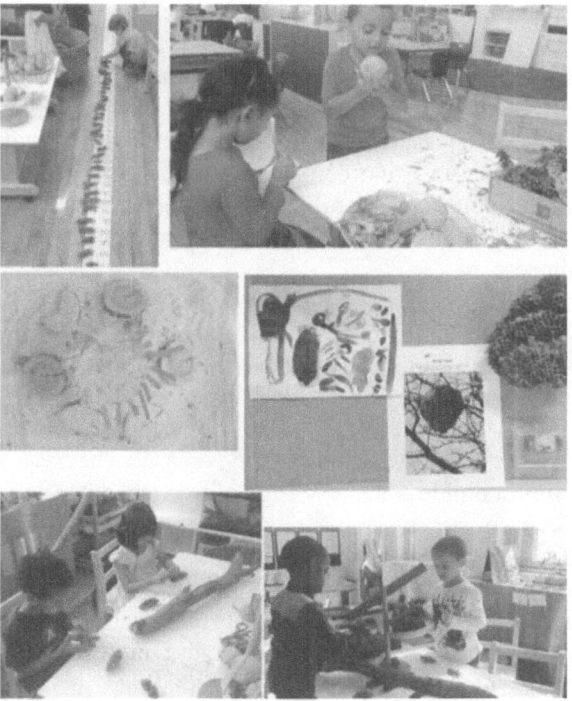

Figure 4.1.

trees, the ELLs follow and participate because they engage in those same experiences.
- Charting children's questions about what they experience related to trees. Questions included "What are the parts of a tree?" and "What are some of the ways the trees are the same, and how are they different?" The answers to these questions are repeatedly investigated and reported on during park excursions, in small- and whole-group investigations.

ELLs benefit from the opportunity to observe the modeling of questions in relation to a topic they are familiar with. Overall, the experiential, integrated, and emergent curriculum tied to a central focus allows for repeated vocabulary in a variety of contexts that stem from children's own activities. This represents an ideal context for language learning for all children including ELLs.

- Art activities to represent children's knowledge about the curriculum topic. As the children discovered more detailed information about the attrib-

utes of trees, their representations became more accurate. Throughout the learning centers, children used colorful pressed leaves for rubbings, printing, and collage. They used twigs to paint with, on, and glue together.
- New vocabulary tying curriculum to the art activities. Words describing parts of a tree, such as seed, pods, roots, branches, leaves, veins, pine cones, pine needles, sap, acorns, bark, limbs, sticks, twigs, fruit, and wood, as well as types of trees, such as pine conifir/evergreen, Osage orange, and London Plane trees, were introduced during read-alouds and reinforced as children worked on their representations in various art pieces and learning centers.

Providing found objects for open-ended exploration throughout the classroom enables both ELL and English-dominant children to develop a shared vocabulary and shared knowledge through hands-on experience.

- Culminating tree sculpture activity. Clay, a cardboard base, and twigs are used to represent children's knowledge of tree attributes and structure and to reflect their developing understandings of similarities and differences. Before the activity, the teacher reads books such as *One Tree* by Marie Tabler and *Call Me Tree* by Maya Gonzalez to direct children's attention to the parts of a tree. At the art table the teacher demonstrates how to form the clay with hands and then shape it more precisely with the plastic knives. Finally, real twigs collected from the park are attached to form branches.

This type of culminating activity that connects learned concepts with a 3-D representation could be used for any topic.

- Action words are repeated to describe children's use of the clay. Vocabulary includes "roll," "pinch," "pull," and "pound."

Language related to a specific function is more easily integrated as stored vocabulary (Halliday, 1976). In addition, the tree vocabulary the children hear in multiple contexts is reiterated as the teacher asks children to think about how to make their tree unique. As a backdrop to this activity the teacher displays prints of tree-themed professional artwork throughout the classroom.

Providing a variety of visual representations of the curriculum enables ELLs equal access. Similarly, integrating concrete materials into art, science, math, and social studies that connect to the unit of study allows ELLs to communicate their ideas about the topic through art.

USING COLLECTIVE ACTIVITIES TO ENGAGE ALL LEARNERS AND SOLIDIFY CLASSROOM COMMUNITY

- Collaborative mural painting. The teacher brings in a two-screen cloth panel and lays first one and then two panels across two tables in the art area, providing space for many children to work at a time. The inspiration for the project is Alma Thomas's painting *Fallen Leaves*, which the teacher projects on a screen within the art area. The teacher provides watercolors and oil pastels in colors like those in the painting. Small-group conversations between peers are supplemented for the ELLs by reference to the colors, shapes, and actions of the large-scale painting as they add to each other's work.

Collective discoveries and collaborative projects support the development of an inclusive classroom community. In addition, these group experiences provide many opportunities for ELLs to hear and practice language while engaged in shared activities with a common goal. The shared perspective supported by this allows for intersubjectivity to develop between ELLs and English-dominant peers, a key dimension of social interaction to enable language development (Rommetveit, 1979). Figure 4.2 depicts the collaborative outdoor and indoor activities.

THE CURRICULUM AS CHILDREN'S COMMON INTERESTS AND SHARED EXPERTISE

Among the ELL children, Amy is particularly engaged in art. As she becomes an increasingly active member of the class, the teacher finds a way to tie curriculum directly to her interests and skills and to shift them to the shared interests of the class. The story that follows describes this process.

Part 1

The children wonder about the animals that live in trees. Some of the children participate in creating a tree trunk around the pretend area by sculpting large cardboard boxes and painting with rollers. Amy observes the activity closely. The pretend area is transformed into a tree trunk with bird, squirrel, and raccoon masks added to enhance the play. The pretend area soon becomes Amy's new favorite place to play. She enjoys dressing up with masks. One day she goes to the art area to make a mask of her own, and her elaborate design quickly draws the attention of her peers.

The class participates in Lesley Koplow's (2008) emotionally responsive bear curriculum, and each child had a teddy bear to take care of. When the teacher asks the class for ideas on how to take care of the bears, some of the

Figure 4.2. Children carry uprooted tree in the park for their classroom as part of inquiry. Image is projected onto Smart Board for children to reference as they create their own representational work of autumn.

children mention that they need clothes. Amy responds by creating clothes for her bear with construction paper and tape.

The other children take notice of her costuming abilities and begin seeking her out for her paper-cutting skills and designs. Soon she is making bear costumes for most of her classmates. Minimal verbal communication occurs during these peer interactions. Amy continues to use one-word phrases and pointing. Her peers try to ensure she understands them with gestures and simple phrases.

Amy's costumes for pretend animals in the dramatic play area, for the bears and other elaborate paper-cutting creations, are highly artistic, and she is proud of her work. The teacher asks Amy if she would like to share her creations during group time. Amy is familiar with the sharing time as it is a repeated classroom routine. At first she declines, and the teacher offers to share it for her, to which she agrees.

Amy's creative use of paper cutting extends to the whole class, and soon the supply of paper is gone. The teacher uses the opportunity to introduce the idea of recycling, and the class embarks on a study of paper.

- Paper-making activity for paper study. The steps for making paper are as follows: (1) Collect paper from recycling bins throughout the school. (2) Rip paper into small pieces or use a paper shredder. (3) Put paper shreds in a blender with two cups of water. (4) Blend for 20 seconds. (5) Pour the pulp into a screen and push through the screen with large felt cloth. (6) Flip the screen over with the remaining layer and let dry.

Part 2

Amy participates enthusiastically in paper making and takes a particular interest in the messing-about table that now contains the shredded paper that will be used for the paper-making activity. One day, Amy takes the shredded paper and brings it to the nearby art area. There she creates an original artwork using paint, glue, and the paper scraps. She first paints on easel paper and then, using glue, adds bits of crumpled paper before it dries. The children, seeing her completed painting, ask her, "How do you do that?"

With the teacher's support Amy creates an area between the easel and the messing-about table and makes a sign to designate it as the area for the paper-painting technique. She then teaches the other children how to use the technique for their own artwork. She now speaks in English phrases, pausing for an extended period between each word. Although this makes regular peer communication difficult, her explanations of her technique are more easily expressed by referring to the necessary actions and materials. Eventually every single child has a paper painting to display atop the previous easel paintings that bordered the classroom.

In this activity, Amy and art are at the center of the community of learners to which she belongs. By the end of the year, Amy is among the many children who bring their parents to admire their work in the "gallery." But this time, Amy sometimes chooses English to explain and describe her art to her mother (who speaks English).

Analysis

In this classroom, art provides multiple entry points and scaffolds for the ELLs to participate in the curriculum and the community of learners. In September, seeing their own creations adorning the classroom walls alongside their peers demonstrates that the classroom space is their own. Their art products serve as a symbolic representation of their equal belonging in the classroom.

Through observing the students' actions with materials, the teacher can glimpse thought processes that could not be expressed in English. This provides cues for how to engage children like Amy. At the same time, the shared manipulations and experimentations with concrete objects enables nonverbal communication and common understandings to occur among the ELLs and their English-dominant peers. Integrating art into dramatic play, literacy, science, and math as a means for engaging with the curriculum enables ELLs to particple fully in the community of learners.

Lev Vygotsky (1978) contends that learning occurs within each learner's zone of proximal development. In addition to language-based assistance from experts, children use cultural artifacts, tools that represent the values of their society to provide support for their eventual mastery of culturally valued skills. The culture of this classroom creates an environment rich with cultural artifacts that could be used by ELLs to master the skills valued within this classroom. Initiated by the teacher and supported by the children these values included experimentation, self-expression, collaboration, and an understanding of the connections between related areas.

Open-ended materials, found objects, and pictograph signs that represented either the child themselves or their understandings of the world served as cultural artifacts to support the children's exploration and eventual mastery of these valued skills. In addition, weaving art-making processes throughout all subject areas provided a scaffolding for all the children, one that was as accessible to Amy and the other ELLs as it was to their peers.

In conclusion, art can be used to provide an entry point into the curriculum using concrete objects and hands-on experimentation as well as through scaffolding peer communication. In the case of Amy, art enabled a child who was not proficient in the English language to see her skills and interests at the center of the class's learning activities. The activities described in this chapter offer a variety of ways that teachers can use art to form an inclusive kindergarten learning environment for all children. In addition, this chapter suggests that key to the development of English language learners is their full participation in the community of their English-speaking classmates. Art is one way to allow for this participation.

REFERENCES

Bruner, J. (1996). *The culture of education.* Cambridge, MA: Harvard University Press.
Cazden, C. B. (2001). *Classroom discourse: The language of teaching and learning.* Portsmouth, NH: Heinemann.
Halliday, M. A. K. (1976). *System and function in language.* London: Oxford University Press.
Rogoff, B. (2003). *The cultural nature of human development.* New York: Oxford University Press.
Rommetveit, R. (1979). *On the architecture of intersubjectivity.* New York: Plenum.

Vygotsky, L. (1978). *Mind and society: The development of higher mental processes.* Cambridge, MA: Harvard University Press.

TEACHER/CURRICULUM RESOURCES

Curtis, D., & Carter, M. (2015). *Designs for living and learning: Transforming early childhood environments.* St. Paul, MN: Red Leaf Press.
Daly, L., & Beloglovsky, M. (2015). *Loose parts: Inspiring play in young children.* St. Paul, MN: Red Leaf Press.
Edwards, C., & Gandini, L. (1998). *The hundred languages of children: The Reggio Emilia experience in transformation.* Greenwich, CT: Ablex.
Falk, B., & Darling-Hammond, L. (2012). *Defending childhood: Keeping the promise of early education.* Early Childhood Education Series. New York: Teachers College Press.
Louv, R. (2008). *Last child in the woods: Saving our children from nature-deficit disorder.* Chapel Hill, NC: Algonquin.

CHILDREN'S BOOKS

Dwight, L., & Cheltenham Elementary School kindergartners. (1991). *We are all alike . . . We are all different (Todos somos iguales . . . Todos somos diferentes).* New York: Scholastic.
Gonzalez, M. C. (2014). *Call me tree (Llámame árbol).* New York: Lee & Low.
Katz, K. (2002). *The colors of us.* New York: Henry Holt.
Kostecki-Shaw, J. S. (2011). *Same, same but different.* New York: Henry Holt.
Zobel-Nolan, A., & Sakamoto, M. (2005). *What I like about me!* Pleasantville, NY: Reader's Digest Children's Books.

Chapter Five

Telling Stories after School

Using Photography to Build Literacy and Community

Tabitha Dell'Angelo, Lauren Madden, and
Maureen Hudson

Meeting the needs of children who are recent immigrants and English language learners (ELLs) can be challenging. Nearly one in ten public school students in the United States is an ELL (Ruiz Soto, Hooker, & Batalova, 2015), and ELLs make up the fastest-growing student population (Schenkel, Chao, & Olsen, 2013). Yet many teachers do not have specific preparation in how to teach non-English-speaking students or students with limited English proficiency. And with students coming from a myriad of backgrounds and life experiences, being a truly culturally responsive teacher and creating a classroom that values all students can seem daunting.

This chapter describes an after-school program that utilized photography to enhance literacy skills among students who were recent arrivals to the United States. Specifically, the chapter will (1) provide background and theoretical grounding of the program; (2) describe the program; and (3) offer strategies and discuss unexpected challenges so educators can implement activities in their own classroom.

PHOTOGRAPHY AND LITERACY

Enter most schools and you will hear about literacy instruction or the "literacy block." However, literacy itself is not a subject—it is something much bigger. Paulo Freire encouraged a broader definition of literacy to include the ability to understand both "the word and the world." Literacy includes reading, writing, listening, and speaking, as well as analyzing a wide range of texts that include both print and nonprint texts. This after-school program was an example of utilizing aspects of literacy and applying a framework of narrative inquiry.

Narrative inquiry is an epistemological approach that leverages our innate desire to know and understand ourselves through story (Andrews, Squire, & Tambokou, 2008). The use of photography allowed us to scaffold a way for children to tell their stories without relying solely on the written word. This method invites children to share their experience of the world and participate in one of the most universal human experiences—storytelling.

There is a great tradition of using photography to create narratives that is underutilized by many classroom teachers. Examples such as the work of Dorothea Lange who captured images of the Great Depression; photojournalists who told stories of Vietnam; Harlem Renaissance photographer James Van Der Zee who captured portraits of the emergent African American middle class during the '20s and '30s; or the modern-day Humans of New York movement that seeks to communicate the realities of life today all provide mentor texts for teachers wishing to create this opportunity for their own students.

A review of related literature revealed only a handful of recent studies in which practicing teachers used photography as a tool for engaging children. Yet, in the studies that exist, we see evidence that photography can be a powerful tool for teaching and learning. For example, Sharon Switzer (2009) examined multimodal literacy experiences of three- and four-year-old children from financially disadvantaged Brazilian immigrant families. Switzer found that families using photographic images alongside other media (e.g., music, drama, and video) helped children connect to their families and home culture. This work suggests that teachers and schools should recognize these multiple forms of literacy in children's developing narratives.

Similarly, Steve Kroeger and colleagues (2004) used PhotoVoice coupled with interviews with a group of middle school students who presented at-risk behaviors. After completing an ongoing PhotoVoice exploration, the middle schoolers were both more connected to the school community and better engaged in learning. Kristin Cook and Gayle Buck (2010) found that middle schoolers could identify socioscientific issues within their schools and surrounding communities through using PhotoVoice as well. Taken together, these studies suggest that engaging children (including those deemed "at risk" or who are nonnative English speakers) with photography can result in increased student engagement and connections.

THE PROGRAM

In a small community in New Jersey where schools have been struggling with underperformance and threatened with state takeovers, teachers are working hard to meet the needs of all students. The activities and lessons discussed in this chapter are based on a program led by teacher candidates from a local college, in partnership with an after-school program. The after-school program focused on supporting students new to the United States by using photography to improve literacy skills among the participants. The teacher candidates led the after-school program once weekly for about an hour over the course of six weeks.

PHOTOGRAPHY-BASED CLASSROOM STRATEGIES

For students with limited English proficiency, photography is a powerful medium for developing oral and written literacy skills.[1] Literacy skills can be advanced and improved without relying on prior knowledge of extensive vocabulary. Instead, these practices can capitalize on vocabulary in a child's native language while also building his or her vocabulary in English. The following activities, successfully developed and implemented in the after-school program, require students to engage in high-level literacy practices, work collaboratively, and produce high-quality work.

Focus

Try to help children focus their gaze and guide their thinking about the photos, but still leave them lots of room to give their own ideas. Ask students to "read" images by examining the details of a photograph and describing what they see. These discussions tap into children's prior knowledge and may help to inspire their storytelling and writing as well as prepare them for taking their own photos.

Portraits

Have students view a wide variety of portraits. Find portraits of political figures, ordinary people, celebrities, and so forth. Put all the photos down on a table, and ask the children to sort them. Children may sort them by gender, age, or some other variable. It really doesn't matter what they decide. After they sort, ask them to describe why they sorted them the way they did.

Teachers can also ask students to guess who these people are based on the photo. What does the photo tell you? Have students think about the intention of the photographer. Who took this photo? Was he or she an insider or outsider? How do we know? Ask students where the camera is. Where are the subjects looking? As an extension activity, students can frame self-portraits or take portraits of one another or family members.

Building Vocabulary and Using Evidence

Find photos from past eras. You can do a Google search to find a photography book by someone such as Helen Levitt or Dorothea Lange or a site such as the Library of Congress's American Memory.[2] Students can also do something as simple as make lists of everything they notice in a photograph. This practice is about both noticing and building vocabulary.

Next, students will make inferences about when this picture was taken and provide evidence for their guess. Teachers should ask students to think about what the photo tells them about the people in it. Look at the expressions on their faces, their poses, the background, and so forth. How does each detail contribute to how the portrait makes you feel? Teachers support students in understanding that the very same picture could make some people feel happy and others sad (or any other range of emotions).

Perspective Taking

Students choose an object and take a photo of it from six inches away, from six feet away, from below, and from above (see figure 5.1 for an example of one perspective). All four pictures are displayed, and students discuss how the different perspectives communicate a different feeling, tone, and message. Notice that when the camera is low, it might make the person or object look more powerful, while when the camera is higher, it might do the opposite.

Telling a Story

Students take photos and sequence them in a way they feel tells a story. Next, they bring these photos to class and trade with a partner. Each partner examines the photo and decides what story they feel the photo is telling. After a few minutes, partners tell the story they feel their photo conveys. Then they debrief about how their partner's analysis agrees or disagrees with their own intent as the photographer. The next step is for the students to write a story that goes either with their own picture or with a picture by one of their classmates. This work is inherently collaborative and provides a communication context between students that can bridge understanding between students with varying levels of English proficiency.

Figure 5.1. *Photo by Destiny De La Rosa.*

LESSONS LEARNED FROM IMPLEMENTING THE PROGRAM

As with many after-school programs, especially in schools with challenges, getting the initial organization off the ground can be difficult. These challenges are worth mentioning because they are likely to happen in other contexts too and they should not be a deterrent to implementing innovative programming. Unexpected challenges in this program included the student population, supplies, and even the weather.

Lesson 1

> Go with the flow. There are not enough high-quality and innovative after-school programs. More children want them than you can serve.

On the first day, upon arrival the school staff explained that while the program would be run with the after-school English language program, it would also have a group of students who were native English speakers but "really excited about photography." This was explained with about three minutes between arrival to the school and walking up the stairs to the classroom to meet the children. There was no opportunity to discuss whether this was a good idea or plan for this change. Sixteen smiling fourth- and fifth-grade faces awaited the beginning of six weeks of fun.

Upon greeting the class it was almost obvious on-site who was who. All of the non-English-speaking students sat on one side of the room with their ELL teacher. The other side of the room had primarily African American students and one white student. For most of that day the native English-speaking students did all the talking. They would often interrupt or answer for the ELLs. Even among elementary-aged children, these microaggressions were common. These became opportunities to gently point them out and encourage the offending students to be more mindful of their words while also encouraging the other students to advocate for themselves.

These prompts seemed to work. Once, a young girl from Guatemala, Maria,[3] was interrupted by another girl, Sienna. Sienna began to answer a question for Maria. One of the teachers asked Sienna to give Maria a moment to think about how she wanted to answer. Maria smiled, took a moment, and after answering the question explained to Sienna that sometimes she needs more time to "figure out the English." She shared that she gets nervous because she sometimes knows the answer in Spanish but teachers and friends don't give her enough time to say what she means in English. Sienna listened to Maria and then said, "I didn't think of that, but it makes sense."

Over the weeks, not only did the children begin sitting together in our class but also teachers from the school reported that they would interact and "high five each other in the hallways." This was an unintended but positive consequence of having the additional native-speaking students in our program.

Lesson 2

> More supplies are needed than you think. Make an exhaustive list long before the program is to start. Solicit donations, double-check supplies, and get extra everything.

Programs like this one need cameras but not just cameras. The principal shared that the school had a few digital cameras that were purchased and not being used. The program organizers solicited donations via e-mail and Facebook. The advent of decent phone cameras and less expensive digital cameras apparently left quite a few friends and relatives with plenty of cameras they were willing to donate.

Unfortunately, it was not until a few days prior to the program that it was realized that generosity stopped at memory cards. Almost every camera was missing the memory card. This came as a complete surprise to the faculty supervisor and teacher candidates. The night before, the faculty supervisor spent more than two hundred dollars on memory cards and batteries.

Last, the program's culminating project was a photography exhibit. Each student created a collage of photos and text. But to show these works at the exhibit, they needed to be enlarged and printed, in color, and laminated. Also, the students created invitations for their event and distributed them widely. That meant cardstock and ink—a lot of ink. Poor planning had a real monetary cost. It would be a good idea to create a clear budget ahead of time and find out what supplies the school is willing to donate. Another option is helping a teacher write a grant proposal through DonorsChoose.org or another teacher-friendly organization. Also, once high-ticket items such as memory cards are purchased once, they do not need to be purchased again.

Lesson 3

> Check the weather. Have a backup plan.

For six weeks, the children worked hard. They became photographers and writers, and they were proud. Their enthusiasm was especially evident when creating and writing out invitations to the exhibit. They wanted to invite everyone. It was going to be an epic celebration of these children. The program organizers secured a beautiful space near to the school that was easily accessible.

Then, on the day of the exhibit a huge storm hit: torrential rains, colder-than-normal temperatures, and flooded streets. The gallery space looked beautiful. The stark white walls and big, front gallery windows allowed the students' work to shine. Unfortunately, the weather kept many people away. A few teachers, parents, and students came by. A few people came in off the street; they may have been trying to escape the rain, but they stayed and shared their impressions of the student work as well. One teacher asked that her photo be taken in front of all the work that her students produced. She wanted to make sure they knew that she was there and that she was proud of them.

In retrospect, more than one night to display work needed to be scheduled in case that night was not convenient for everyone or, in this case, unexpected weather events keep people away. Perhaps the project team could have arranged to set up the exhibit in the school so that the students could share their work with even more of their teachers and friends.

CONCLUSION

All of the students—the new immigrants and the native-born students—suffer from others defining who they are. They are the "urban kids," "black kids," "Spanish kids," "immigrant kids," and so forth. This project allowed students to reclaim their identity and define themselves. They created their representation by using specific photography techniques that tell the story they want to share about themselves and pair the images with text.

Creating the space for children to develop photo narratives allowed students to express and define themselves and to use narrative to tell their own stories rather than being defined by others or by an outside narrative that may exist about them. Over the six weeks, the students' literacy skills and confidence grew. One unintentional positive outcome was the social benefits from participation in the program. Through learning together, experimenting with photography, and creating the photo narratives the children became a community of friends and artists. The work they created allowed them to connect with one another as well as with their families and teachers in an authentic way.

NOTES

1. This section is taken from Dell'Angelo (2014).
2. https://memory.loc.gov/ammem/index.html.
3. All names throughout are pseudonyms.

REFERENCES

Andrews, M., Squire, C., & Tambokou, M. (Eds.). (2008). *Doing narrative research*. London: Sage.

Cook, K., & Buck, G. (2010). PhotoVoice: A community-based socioscientific pedagogical tool. *Science Scope, 33*(7), 35–39.

Dell'Angelo, T. (2014, December 1). Literacy through photography for English language learners. *Edutopia*. Retrieved from https://www.edutopia.org/.

Kroeger, S., Burton, C., Comarata, A., Combs, C., Hamm, C., Hopkins, R., & Kouche, B. (2004). Student voice and critical reflection: Helping students at risk. *Teaching Exceptional Children, 36*(3), 50–57.

Ruiz Soto, A. G., Hooker, S., & Batalova, J. (2015). *States and districts with the highest number and share of English language learners*. Washington, DC: Migration Policy Institute.

Schenkel, J., Chao, J., & Olsen, L. (2013). *Educating English language learners: Grantmaking strategies for closing America's other achievement gap*. Portland, OR: Grantmakers for Education.

Switzer, S. C. (2009). Multiple modes of communication of young Brazilian children: Singing, drawing, and English language learning. In M. Narey (Ed.), *Making Meaning* (pp. 133–152). Pittsburgh: Springer.

Chapter Six

Bilingualism and Project Arts-Based Learning

Laura Felleman Fattal

Between the years 1990 and 2010, the population of students with limited English proficiency in the United States increased by 80 percent with a concentrated growth in 10 states (Lucas & Villegas, 2013). The importance of the demographic change underscores the urgency to address new bilingual learners. Project-based learning, a type of inquiry-based learning, requires engagement and collaboration and is open to students' inquiries and challenges. The sustained engagement has been shown to improve motivation, attitude toward learning, and work habits (Barron & Darling-Hammond, 2008).

Bilingual students' cognitive, affective, and social engagement in academic content is expedited through project arts-based learning. Student-centered pedagogy, such as project arts-based learning, focuses on realistic and complex tasks resulting in a presentation or performance that has proven to advance bilingual students' achievement (Barron & Darling-Hammond, 2008). With a lens to improve bilingual student academic content and language acquisition, a series of project arts-based learning experiences are examined and analyzed in an urban, bilingual, third-grade elementary school classroom.

I, the university researcher, worked collaboratively with the school principal and second- and third-grade teachers in a northern New Jersey urban elementary school. The elementary school had one or more bilingual classrooms at each grade level, one through six, in a school with a total population of more than 1,100 students; many of the children's families and the children themselves came from Mexico, the Dominican Republic, Peru, and Ecuador. During spring 2015 the second-grade students had interventions that included theater, movement, music, and visual arts instruction aligned with science, math, language arts, and social studies learning. The focus of the fall 2015 arts interventions was a third-grade bilingual classroom where two-thirds of the students had been second graders who participated in the spring arts-based learning activities.

The third-grade students were encouraged to communicate through their language of choice, in this case, English or Spanish, with their peers or teacher. Being that language is an expression of culture, the choice of language used at a precise moment in learning or creating reflects a richer and deeper cognitive experience. Translanguaging is the discourse practice of bilinguals that transcends socially constructed language structures to engage diverse, multiple meaning-making systems (Garcia, 2009). Allowing students to "translanguage" is a pedagogical resource that uses bilingualism as a resource, rather than a hindrance. This practice allows the learners to construct their cognitive experience and share it with participants using the vocabulary they already possess (Garcia, 2009).

The WIDA (World-class Instructional Design and Assessment) consortium has created "Can Do Descriptors" for bilingual learners that provide a framework for language learning that includes sensory, graphic, and interactive supports such as real objects, illustrations, physical movement, number lines, and varied student groupings evident in the third-grade arts intervention discussed in this chapter. Jim Cummins (2001) attends to the importance of human relationships and the positive use of translanguaging, the use of the native language and English, in interactive communication for bilingual student success in the classroom. Current research on the metacognitive benefits of brain elasticity in dual-language learners is reinforced by communicative strategies noted by Cummins and sensory and graphic supports evident through involvement in the arts.

THE AMBIANCE OF SCHOOL

Families and visitors are greeted by a warm cordiality when entering the elementary school where the project arts-based learning in bilingual classes is located; Spanish and English is used interchangeably. The guards, custodians, administrative staff, and teaching staff are amicable, and the experienced bilingual administrator has a deep regard for the emotional intelligence of her students and faculty. She intersperses her spoken and written language with high-leverage words to increase student vocabularies in casual and formal situations. She is a great believer in the power and humanity of the arts to enrich the whole child.

ARTS INTERVENTIONS/LANGUAGE ARTS/SHADOW PUPPETS

As an introduction to the third-grade students who did not have arts interventions in second grade and a refresher to the students who experienced arts interventions the previous semester, the researcher facilitates a shadow-puppet-making class. The objective of the shadow-puppet lesson is to increase the variety of English and Spanish verbs that the children would employ in their writing and speaking. The researcher reads the story *Because* (2007) about the modern dancer Isadora Duncan retold by the ballet dancer Mikhail Baryshnikov and illustrator Vladimir Radunsky.

The purposeful selection of the illustrated book depicting exaggerated quotidian movements of sliding, twirling, walking, jumping, and stretching acts as an accessible visual model for the children's shadow puppets. The action verbs read aloud detailing the movements of the book's characters provides the children with auditory reinforcement of the action words.

The classroom, arranged with five tables with four or five children at each table, creates an ease with group work and partnering in project arts-based learning. After the researcher reads the book, assisted by the bilingual classroom teacher, the assistant teacher, and the resource teacher, the students are given thin, white foam paper to draw their selected pose inspired by an action word from the story.

The students use the whole seven-by-four-inch foam paper to draw the action figure, cut it out, and then, if there is enough time, to cut off the limbs of the puppet. The limbs are then reattached with paper fasteners enabling the puppets to more vigorously move to enact various poses (see figure 6.1). The children then attach a tongue depressor on the back of the puppet with masking tape as a handle to hold the puppet. The researcher brings a white sheet and a flashlight to class for a stage curtain and lighting for the shadow puppets' performance.

Table by table the children come up to the white sheathed table and with the researcher sit on the floor behind the white sheet. The other children look on as each child moves his or her puppet in the action that was depicted in the story, and in a sentence, orally describes the puppet's action. One girl writes, "Then I was balancing on the bicycle. . . . I could twist a little with the bicycle . . . I can skate and roll." The children in the audience are gleeful in anticipating doing the same activity as their friends.

The intended outcome of the arts intervention, a project arts-based learning experience, is multifold: (a) to hear and understand the illustrated storybook; (b) to manipulate art materials to show choreographed movement; (c) to visualize new actions words/verbs; (d) to verbalize English and Spanish words of specific movements/actions of the puppets; (e) to work and perform as a small group in the puppet show; and (f) to write the selected verbs that described the action of the puppet and can refer, when needed, to the vocabu-

Figure 6.1. Shadow puppets

lary word by looking at the classroom word wall. Without elaborate materials or preparation, student learning can be made visible in its incremental and final stages (Barnett, 2013). The shadow-puppet show is an example of project arts-based learning grounded in social interaction and an authentic performance documented through photography and video extending the reflective component of the learning.

ARTS INTERVENTION/MATH/PROTRACTORS

Planning of interactive learning with hands-on strategies can be facilitated in two languages (Alanis, Salinas-Gonzalez, & Arreguin-Anderson, 2015). With third graders, facilitating a math lesson on measuring space, in Spanish and English, is made more accessible through the use of protractors, small multisided wood blocks, and pipe cleaners (see figure 6.2). The children measure the angle of the corners of the irregularly shaped blocks and then the opening between the legs of their chairs, thereby being introduced to positive and negative space.

The children write down what they measure and the numerical angle of the measurement. The math lesson, which lasts for more than an hour, requires the assistance of the adult teachers in the room due to the necessary movement in measuring physical objects. The culminating measuring activity is to take one of the measured sides of the wood block and translate that angle into a shape shown with a bent pipe cleaner. The children's pipe cleaners in their various shapes are then scotch-taped to the wooden block making a small sculpture.

The light wood block and the colored pipe cleaner with the marked angle is in fact a unique sculpture that each student had assembled. The oral language production associated with this project is prompted by the sculpture itself. Each student is asked to describe where he or she found the angle, how it was measured, and how it was translated into the linear pipe-cleaner form; the sculpture provided visual clues and references (Alanis, Salinas-Gonzalez, Arreguin-Anderson, 2015).

ART INTERVENTIONS/MATH/POLYGONS—TANGRAMS

Tangrams are ancient Chinese puzzles that are still in use today. A tangram begins with a square, which is then cut into seven standard pieces; each piece is called a tan. All seven tans must be used in creating a picture where the tans must touch but not overlap. In the book *Grandfather Tang's Story*

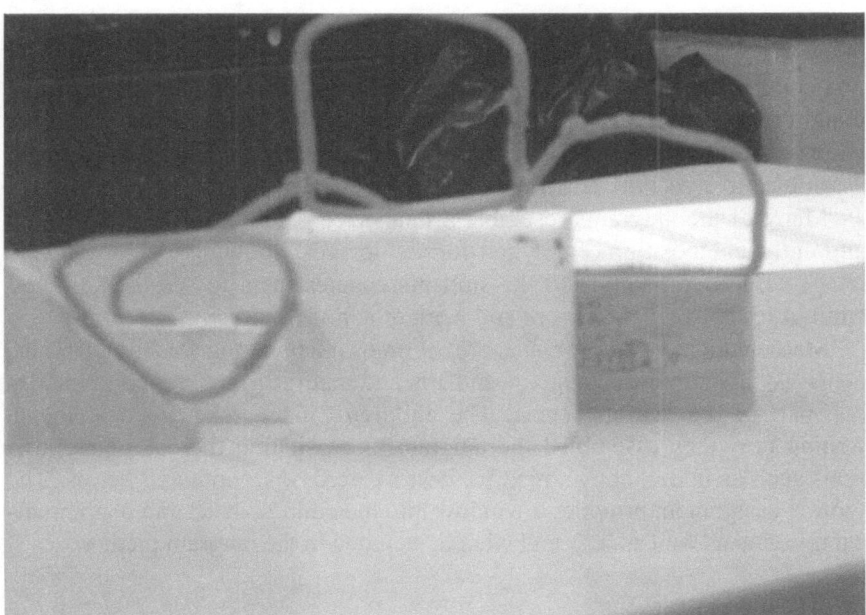

Figure 6.2. Pipe cleaner and wood sculptures

(1990) by Ann Tompert, seven tans create fox fairies that in Chinese folklore have special powers.

The transformation of the tans to create different animals is pivotal to the story that forms the basis of the mathematical learning. Animals are created by placement of the varied-sized and varied-positioned triangles, rectangles, rhombuses, parallelograms, and squares; the slanted sides of some polygons formed human arms or goose necks; squares become tilted human heads; and rearranging the polygon shapes creates a goose, a rabbit, a fox, a lion, a hawk, a squirrel, or a dog.

The inventiveness of the progression of tangram-shaped animals in the fantastic tale is accompanied by an illustration of the actual animal; this encourages children in individualized, fanciful storytelling. The math learning focuses on recognizing patterns and understanding that triangles, rectangles, squares, and other polygons have distinct characteristics regardless of their size and direction.

The teacher distributes green and aqua construction paper for the background of the polygon puzzle and contrasting violet-, beige-, or salmon-colored construction paper for the tangram pieces. Working in cooperative groups, each table of five students is given one animal tangram to create using the original square formatted with adjoining size pieces. A few students cut out their tangrams quickly and with visual acuity re-create the tangram. Other students need assistance in cutting and then placing the correct polygons in place so an animal is formed. The tonally contrasting tangram pieces are glued down on the variously colored construction paper so if one child is uncertain how to juxtapose the tans, other students at the table could quickly recognize the problem and assist him or her. There may be a wide variation in how quickly, carefully, and correctly the tangram pieces are assembled to create the fanciful animals.

Many of the tangrams resemble a Paul Klee painting in their coloration and in the composition of polygon-formed images. Showing a photographed image of a Klee painting to the students enables them to see the aesthetic similarities between their work and work of a modern artist.

Mathematical word problems are, at times, challenging for bilingual students. By assembling a tangram, the arts and math learning are combined as one part of the learning cycle. The children can be asked to describe in writing how they assembled the tangram, necessitating the use of prepositions such as under, above, next to, near to, across, around, and below. The writing assignment provides a window into the child's visual and mathematical thinking as well as how and what is included in the tangram picture.

ARTS INTERVENTION/MATH/CLAY TOYS WITH ANIMAL APPENDAGES

While the researcher reads the children's book *Dream Carver* (2002) by Diana Cohn, illustrated by Amy Córdova, the third graders are asked to follow the narrative that includes both dreams and real events. Mateo, a young boy, watches his father, an accomplished artist, carve toys shaped as animals—pigs, cats, dogs, and goats that he sells at the fiesta market in Mexico. Mateo helps his father carve the toys while his mother and sister paint them.

Mateo dreams of carving his own version of the animals that are in his village and painting them with unusual colors; Mateo even dreams of a pink and gold jaguar. One day he goes off by himself after helping his father and starts carving his own animals; the wood seems to inspire him so that the sculptural toys just spring from the wood.

Watching the researcher slowly read the book aloud to the class provides time for the children to examine the very colorful and clearly outlined illustrations. The clarity of the pictures provides easy access to the story line, which includes a simmering family conflict. The math-centered arts intervention focuses on pricing the new clay (a substitute for carving in wood) toys that the third graders will build to be sold at a Mexican fiesta. The math problem requires the children to price their own unique artifacts.

The researcher distributes different colors of clay to each child and lays out five small colorful plastic insects that are to be an inspiration for added appendages/antennas to the clay animal toys. An individual aesthetic is encouraged since every student at the table has clay in a different color and chooses a different part of the plastic insect to augment his or her toy (see figure 6.3).

Since the father in the story made his living from selling these toys, the math learning requires that each table, in a group decision, put a price on each toy animal at the table. How to decide if one clay animal is worth more than another is not an easy decision. In the second- and third-grade classrooms, there are number lines that are visual aids for students to see the sequence of the numbers. Project-based learning encourages real-world problem solving (Vega, 2012). The authentic assessment of this project incorporates artistic and mathematical components.

The students initially price their clay animals the same price. Then with more decision making the students decide that larger and more detailed clay animals should cost more than smaller and plainer ones. The students have to figure out how many toys of the same price they would have to make to equal $100. The children need to use multiplication or addition to have the cost of all the clay toys at their table equal $100, thereby making real-world financial decisions. Project-based learning requires that children have control over

Figure 6.3. Clay animals

their learning and that teachers and coaches act as facilitators of inquiry and reflection (Vega, 2012). Displaying the student work enhances the learning environment with a student-centered aesthetic.

SUGGESTIONS

Professional development workshops on project arts-based learning in schools reinforce the intrinsic creativity of teachers and dispel a caution and hesitancy to engage in the arts.

Recommended by Tamara Lucas and Ana Maria Villegas (2013) as part of their framework for linguistically responsive teaching (LRT), instructional scaffolding practices can include extralinguistic supports, adaptation of written texts, adaptation of teachers' oral language, and clear instructions. Scaffolding instruction requires an ease and comfort with varied instructional strategies, an acquired expertise.

Novice and experienced teachers will benefit from interactive professional development workshops that might be best organized with the arts teachers in the school or across grade levels and subject areas. Planned collaborations between art and music and classroom teachers can provide learning scenarios to redouble vocabulary learning and expand math, social studies, science, and language understanding using diverse media. Christian Faltis and Jamal Abedi (2013) discuss extraordinary pedagogies for working with nondominant students underscoring the agency of learners and constructive action: they would like to have teachers become aware of themselves as practitioners and to expand an understanding of narrative inquiry- and arts-based learning for posing questions and agency in learning.

CONCLUSIONS

Project arts-based classrooms create artifacts that are both anchors and springboards for academic discussion. The framework for the project arts-based learning experiences for the third-grade bilingual classroom include the following: (a) empathetic and humanizing story books—see children's books in the reference section and consider *The Mitten* by Jan Brett (1989) and *Blockhead: The Life of Fibonacci* (2010) by Joseph D'Agnese and illustrated by John O'Brien—that have linkages with grade-appropriate language arts and math learning; (b) essential math standards that are introduced and reinforced through tactical arts-based projects; (c) authentic real-world problems and connections to measure and visualize space, to recognize the essential properties of polygons are unrelated to their size and direction, and to accurately price individual and groups of artifacts; (d) embedded oral and written language practice; (e) fluid transitions between core content areas and aesthetic arts-based conversations; and (f) a final performance or presentation. Displaying student work in its formative and completed state underlined the importance of the children's production, their visual and academic learning.

Pride of ownership was evident in the third-grade bilingual classroom but is also evident in all classrooms where student work is displayed; the posting of student work allows the student artists to revisit what they have created, which encourages new ideas for future projects. In addition, exhibited individual and group projects in the classroom or online prompt a family/school connection; representations of academic learning can be made visible to multilingual parents and families attending to the need to engage new Americans in the center of a vibrant educational dialogue.

There is a growing consensus that preparing preservice teachers for inclusive classrooms that include bilingual students needs to involve new student-centered pedagogies. The humanizing effect of the arts provides an engaging and dynamic form of communication to scaffold learning in language and academic content areas. Project arts-based interventions do not have to be created in isolation. We seem to be more creative when we plan together

(Cote, 2012), remarks a teacher after speaking with the art teacher in her school. Close ties between the music teacher and the language arts teacher or interactions of the visual art teacher with the classroom teacher can produce arresting exemplars of student thinking and achievement.

REFERENCES

Alanis, I., Salinas-Gonzalez, l., & Arreguin-Anderson, M. G. (2015). Developing biliteracy with intentional support: Using interactive word walls and paired learning. *Young Children, 70*(4), 46–51.
Barnett, M. (2013). The arts as a bridge to literacy. *Principal*, special supplement. Retrieved from http://www.naesp.org/.
Barron, B., & Darling-Hammond, L. (2008, October 8). Powerful learning: Studies show deep understanding derives from collaborative methods. *Edutopia*. Retrieved from https://www.edutopia.org/inquiry-project-learning-research.
Cote, J. (2012). Arts-based education and creativity. *Action in Teacher Education, 32*(5–6), 126–143.
Cummins, J. (2001). Empowering minority students: A framework for introduction. *Harvard Educational Review, 71*(4), 649–675.
Faltis, C., & Abedi, J. (2013). Extraordinary pedagogies for working within school settings serving nondominant students. *Review of Research in Education, 37*, vii–xi.
Garcia, O. (2009). *Bilingual education in the 21st century: A global perspective*. London: Wiley/Basil Blackwell.
Lucas, T. (Ed.). (2011). *Teacher preparation for linguistically diverse classrooms: A resource for teacher educators*. New York: Routledge.
Lucas, T., & Villegas, A. M. (2013). Preparing linguistically responsive teachers: Laying the foundation in preservice teacher education. *Theory into Practice, 52*(2), 98–109.
Vega, V. (2012, December 3). Project-based learning research review. *Edutopia*. Retrieved from https://www.edutopia.org/pbl-research-learning-outcomes.

CHILDREN'S BOOKS

Baryshnikov, M., & Radunsky, V. (2007). *Because*. New York: Simon & Schuster Children's Publishing.
Cohn, D., & Córdova, A. (2002). *Dream carver*. San Francisco: Chronicle.
Tompert, A. (1990). *Grandfather Tang's story*. New York: Crown.

WEBSITE

WIDA Can Do Descriptors. https://www.wida.us/standards/CAN_DOs.

Chapter Seven

Photovoice as a Vehicle for Supporting Environmental Literacy and Language Acquisition

Marissa E. Bellino, Jennifer D. Adams, and Joanna Higgins

Children and adolescents are inherently engaged in their experiences. As a part of growing and developing, learning is continuous as students interact with others in their communities and schools. For emerging bilingual students, these interactions also include the learning of new language and culture. Using approaches in the classroom that support critical dialogues not only helps emerging bilinguals to become more fluent in languages and cultures but also provides them with a lens to reflect on their lived experience in ways that can foster civic engagement and deeper integration into their lived communities.

As a critical and participatory pedagogy, photovoice provides such a platform for bilingual children and adolescents to study their contexts and critically analyze their lived realities. Cogenerating a multicultural pedagogical experience with all students, teachers can use photovoice as a tool to build collective knowledge as well as address content and language objectives needed to support emerging bilinguals.

This chapter begins with an overview of photovoice as a participatory research methodology with a strong focus on its ability to address issues of environmental and social justice/injustice. The bulk of the chapter is dedicated to presenting a series of stages for developing a meaningful photovoice project in any classroom. Challenges and ethical considerations when designing a photovoice project are addressed throughout this section.

A brief description of a project with children in Wellington, New Zealand, provides an example of one enactment of photovoice with a diverse group of students. The organization and structure of the project is highlighted to showcase how children connect with their surroundings, learn content in meaningful contexts, and raise social and environmental issues. The chapter concludes with a discussion of four key components of photovoice that support both social and academic language development for emerging bilinguals.

PHOTOVOICE: AN OVERVIEW OF THEORY AND PROCESS

The photovoice concept and method is designed to enable people to create and discuss photography as a means of catalyzing personal and community change (Wang, Cash, & Powers, 2000). As such, photovoice can be used as a pedagogical tool in a classroom to investigate students' local communities, while developing research skills and critical thinking. Local environments can be examined and documented through this participatory methodology in which people identify, represent, and enhance their community through images.

With its origins in critical theory and pedagogy (Freire, 2000), feminist theory (Smith, 1987), and participatory approaches to documentary photography, photovoice has three key aims: (1) to enable marginalized groups to record and reflect their community's strengths and concerns; (2) to promote critical dialogue and knowledge production about important community issues through large- and small-group discussion of photographs; and (3) to communicate concerns with policy makers (Wang & Burris, 1997; Wang, 1999).

Theoretical Groundings

Photovoice emerged out of reproductive and community health research and has now been adapted to a variety of new contexts including work with youth and children. This is primarily due to its embedded participatory and emancipatory ideologies that make it an ideal tool for illuminating and addressing issues of social and environmental injustice. Previous applications of photovoice have addressed issues of social inequality as experienced by youth living in urban environments (Bellino & Adams, 2014), cultural and social identity of youth (Faircloth, Hynds, Jacob, Green, & Thompson, 2016; Luttrell, 2010), exploring children's play (Berinstein & Magalhaes, 2009), youth civic engagement (Pritzker, LaChapelle, & Tatum, 2012), and youth empowerment (Strack, Magill, & McDonagh, 2004).

The approach of photovoice draws heavily upon the work of Paulo Freire (2000) and his view that all people hold deep knowledge about the world through their personal experiences. Speaking and sharing about these experiences can cultivate an analytical orientation toward roots of injustice in the hopes of transforming oppressive structures. Feminist theory suggests that those who have voice have power, and as such, when marginalized populations are given an opportunity to voice their knowledge of experience, this can enhance their public presence, thus influencing policy. The New Zealand photovoice project presented in this chapter draws upon these critical and feminist orientations to address socioenvironmental issues in communities. The intersecting theoretical and conceptual frameworks that have informed this application of photovoice include critical pedagogies of place (Gruenewald, 2003), socioecological justice (Furman & Gruenewald, 2004), and youth participatory action research (Cahill, 2007; Cammarota & Fine, 2008). Critical pedagogy of place is a blending of place-based learning and critical pedagogy advocating for learning locally to connect learning to students' everyday lives (Gruenewald, 2003).

Socioecological justice brings together social justice education with an understanding that environmental issues prevalent today are a result of our current political economy and that these issues are disproportionately felt by those with the least economic power (Furman & Gruenewald, 2004). Finally, youth participatory action research (YPAR) is rooted in a belief that research with and by young people can address issues that are important to them, can create a democratic and participatory classroom community, can privilege many ways of knowing, and is emergent and contingent.

The Photovoice Process

Caroline Wang (2006) presents a series of steps for conducting photovoice to mobilize community action. Here, these steps are modified and developed for classroom practice and described in this section as a series of essential and optional stages that both the teacher and students move through. Presented below are brief descriptions about each stage embedded with multiple points of considerations one should address when deciding to use photovoice.

It should be noted that because photovoice is a participatory methodology and there are many levels at which participation can occur, photovoice lends itself nicely to a variety of adaptations. Shared decision making in the scope and direction of a project can allow for greater buy-in from students but might make for less teacher control at the start, which can feel unsettling at times (Bellino, 2015). Every decision made will affect the outcome of a project and engagement by students.

Planning

As with any classroom project, careful planning is important to a successful outcome. First, establish your goals and objectives for photovoice. As there are many ways that a photovoice project can be conducted, consideration should be given to number of students; how students will take pictures (e.g., cameras, video, or phones); number of images each participant will take; how images will be stored, organized, and shared with others; how groups will be arranged; what questions will be used during critical dialogues; how critical dialogues will be modeled and facilitated; and the final product you want individuals or groups to create.

Introduction of Project to Students

Students may not be familiar with photovoice so you can include in your planning how you will introduce the project to students. This can be done by reading about similar photovoice projects, viewing project websites and other final products of related photovoice projects, and most importantly, by introducing the theme, goals, expectations, and time line of the project. The introduction is also a good time to explain to students the rationale behind a particular theme that was chosen (the importance of it to you, them, and others) and to allow students to add their own goals and expectations.

Since photo taking is central to the project, you can do some activities to help focus students on language and images—for instance, have them brainstorm to generate words of the kinds of pictures they might take, write and share a reflection around the theme of the project, complete a graphic organizer, or look at similar photos and come up with words and short phrases to describe them.

Ethics: Safety, Consent, and Power

The introduction is also a good time to address some of the ethical issues associated with photovoice. First, safety is paramount. Since students might be doing some of the work outside of the classroom, emphasize being aware of their surroundings and that feeling safe is more important than taking photographs. Safety in class is also important. During the critical dialogues students share and discuss sensitive issues. It is important to establish clear guidelines for listening, respect, and confidentiality. It is also important to consider your school's policy about informed consent. Students may need parental permission to participate in the activity.

Taking pictures is a big responsibility, and students should understand that if they take pictures of others, especially outside of the class, they should ask permission before photographing, especially if individuals can be identified in the photo. And all permission for display/publication of photos must be obtained in advance. For example, you may want to have an exhibit that showcases students' work or publish a booklet with students' stories and images; this can be empowering for emerging bilinguals. Permission can be obtained by simply adding a consent page on which students obtain the signatures of the people they photograph.

Taking photos of others places the photographer in a position of power where their interpretation of people and images are subjectively situated. Caroline Wang and Yanique Redwood-Jones (2001) recommend creating a brochure that outlines the photovoice project (i.e., goals and how photos will be used) that students can hand out to photo subjects and other community members while out taking pictures.

After each picture-taking session/day, debrief with students and ask if they had any situations or concerns that came up. It is imperative to continually discuss the methodology and ethics of a photovoice project with students and address any issues as they arise.

Practice Photovoice

Taking students on a brief class outing to take a few pictures around a theme can be useful before sending students out on their own. For example, go to a local park or even around your school and have students practice taking different kinds of pictures with a specific theme or focus. Have them practice asking permission if they are taking pictures of people that can be identifiable in the photos. The photo practice excursion should be followed by a debrief where students reflect on the experience and discuss any questions, issues, or concerns that arose. You can also practice the questions for the critical dialogues (see Voicing Photos through Critical Dialogues) with a few images as a whole group or in small groups, have students select one photo and write a brief description, or generate a list of words as to why they took that picture and how it is connected to the theme.

Picture Taking and Sharing

As previously mentioned there are many decisions to make about how to structure a photovoice project. While many decisions can be made as a collective, having a sense of how students will take and share their images is going to be an important consideration. For example, if students are taking pictures on their phones, do they have enough memory to store them and do they have the means to get them from their phone to a computer, or is that necessary for the final product? How will images be shared with other group members? Will you use a cloud-based storage site or create a web page for each participant on a shared site where images can be uploaded? Do you have the computer access and capacity for all participants over multiple days? These are all important questions to consider.

The number of images can be decided before or as a collective, and there can be flexibility in how many pictures. The purpose of photovoice is not to take a lot of pictures but rather to take pictures that have meaning and a sense of purpose to the individual photographer. Once images have been taken, organized, and prepared for sharing, it is time to begin the critical dialogues.

Voicing Photos through Critical Dialogues

The critical dialogues are what make photovoice different from a photography project. Facilitating and engaging in critical dialogues can be challenging but rewarding, especially for bilinguals, as it gives them the opportunity to combine spoken and written language with visual images of people, places, and objects that are meaningful and important to them. The critical dialogues are a good time to remind students about the importance of good listening, respect, and confidentiality. Decide how you will group students for the dialogues, and use the questions below to help you decide how you will structure the critical dialogue sessions.

For each image the student photographer will answer this series of questions, and yet one of the greatest challenges of this questioning is that it can appear to students to leave little room for dialogue. As students are often set on solely answering the questions, the critical discussions can become a monologue. Students need to know that they can expand and ask new questions during the discussion, making connections to their own lives and pictures and adding new knowledge about issues represented. This is what makes for strong dialogues; however, many students are not practiced in having this level of freedom in classroom discussions, so this will take practice and modeling.

One strategy you can use is to have all students in the group begin by sharing what they see in the picture. This can then generate some initial conversation about the diversity of interpretations and then the picture takers can share what they see and why they took it. Audio recorders are a great tool to use during dialogues as they allow students to capture their thinking, something that will be useful in the analysis stage.

As students go through the series of questions below, any image that doesn't generate a lot of discussion should be removed. Below is one modification of the SHOWeD method questions (Wang & Burris, 1997) used to generate critical dialogues about images. You can add, adjust, or remove questions as you deem necessary and based on the scope of your project and language ability of your students.

- What do you see here?
- Why did you take this picture?
- What is really happening here?
- How does this relate to the class theme?
- How do you relate to this picture? How do other people in the group relate to this picture?

- Why does this condition (problem, strength, concern, or situation) exist?
- Is there any action that this generates? What can we do about it?
- How could this image educate others in our community/policy makers?

Questions to Be Discussed at the End of Sharing All Pictures

- What do some of our pictures have in common?
- Are there any images or issues that are different that stand out?

Analysis of Visual Data

The two final questions above lead to initial analysis of images and generation of themes by students. One method that students can use to conduct an individual analysis of their images is to write personal photovoice narratives. These narratives allow students to select a series of images and voice (from the recordings of their dialogues) a particularly meaningful story. These can be written narratives, or if audio was captured, narratives can be edited and presented as short films.

Regardless of the product of the individual analysis, it can be created in a shared space where all students can access and read or listen to one another's narratives. This allows students to conduct another layer of analysis looking for common themes, patterns, and deviations from patterns within the narratives. After sharing these within the group, each group can select a set of images they wish to share with the whole class.

Sharing of Findings

Individuals or groups can create a final product to share with an audience. In essence, this is the action in participatory action research. The selection of audience is another area that needs to be planned prior, especially if policy makers are going to be invited. Gallery walks, formal presentations, websites, books, and nested discussions are all possible ways of sharing the new knowledge produced by youth. Nested discussions involve one group sharing their images while also facilitating a larger discussion with the class/audience in which all members contribute to building knowledge from the images, as well as individual and collective experiences.

Final Reflections and Development of New Directions for Research

Critical reflection on learning can be done at the end of a project. This allows students to share their experience and is also an opportunity for the teacher to see what big ideas students are taking with them from the project. Depending on the goals of the project, student reflections may focus on content learning or more on the development of skills (e.g., to take pictures, to engage in critical dialogues, to upload images, and to create a website). By design, photovoice is an emergent and iterative process in which there are many points at which to cycle back. Initial picture taking and dialogues can lead to new questions that inspire students to take additional photos in new places or of new things.

PHOTOVOICE: WELLINGTON, NEW ZEALAND

Presented here is an application of photovoice that emerged from a collaboration between a local university in Wellington, New Zealand, and a public elementary school. In this example, photovoice was used to connect science and environmental literacy with social justice. The inception for the project came from the teacher and university faculty members who were interested in seeing how photovoice could facilitate student understanding of stormwater in the local Wellington community.

Overview of the Program

The overarching goal of the project was for students to learn about stormwater in their school, local communities, and larger city. Ten students between nine and eleven years old were selected to participate in this project by their teachers because of their interest in photography and ability to obtain parental consent. Photovoice meetings were held for two hours on four consecutive days during an elective time in the school day. The school provided space in the teachers' lounge and library, where presentations and conversations took place. The final product, as determined by the school community, was for the student group to present about their experience to the whole grade at a Friday assembly.

The Photovoice Project

The purpose of the Wellington photovoice project was to document how students were connecting their science learning around stormwater to larger socioscientific issues in their school and communities. The facilitators introduced photovoice to students as a tool to build knowledge together and connect and discuss what we see, what we know, and how we experience something. On the first day, the facilitators introduced the goals of the project, along with a general overview of photovoice, including some of the ways photovoice was conceptualized for the specific New Zealand project. The facilitators created a student-friendly handout used to document the work of each participant throughout the four-day program. Each student added his or her own personal goal for the project, and the goals were then collectively shared. Below are the modified SHOWeD questions used to generate critical dialogue.

- What do you see here?
- Why did you take this picture?
- What is really happening here?
- How does this relate to our lives?
- Why does this condition exist?
- What can we do about it?
- Where is the science in this picture? How can we connect our learning about stormwater to this picture?
- How could this picture educate others?
- What further questions can we ask about this picture?

Questions to Be Discussed at the End of Sharing All Pictures

- What do some of our pictures have in common?
- Are there any pictures or issues that are different that stand out?

As a large group the students practiced answering each question during a photo elicitation activity of stormwater images. The group discussed five images during the activity, and each student wrote down his or her response for the above questions on an adhesive note and placed it onto a big chart paper dedicated to each question. After discussing each image, the students spent time looking at each question and the different answers provided by their peers. This allowed the group to practice the critical dialogues, to focus their thinking around stormwater-related issues, and to begin to see how each of their ways of responding to questions was a piece of data that could be analyzed. Figure 7.1 shows students working through the opening day of activities.

After the photovoice introduction, we gave the students their task for taking pictures: take pictures of anything they had been learning or thinking about related to stormwater. The facilitators divided the students into pairs; each pair was given a camera that they took turns taking home and taking pictures of their communities. The research team provided the cameras, and the school provided the computers. On the following day, students shared their pictures in pairs, working through the critical dialogue questions. Students exchanged cameras with their partners and the next day repeated the process.

After all the images were shared, each student selected one image to write a short paragraph about using a series of sentence prompts. Students were also given audio recorders with the option of recording their narratives. Each student read their brief narrative to the whole group, and common themes

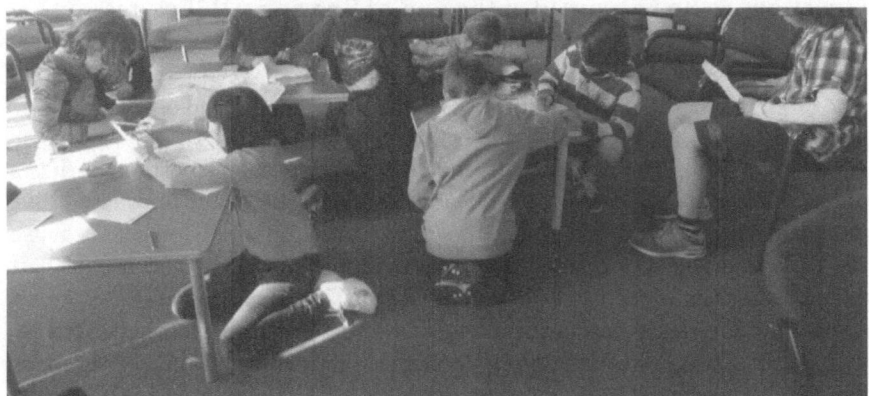

Figure 7.1. Students working on various aspects of the photovoice project.
Photos by Joanna Higgins, August 2015.

that emerged across their photos were discussed. Issues of equitable access to clean drinking water; how water moves, gets dirty, and gets cleaned locally; and how water is used by plants and other organisms were common among the student images.

Many students made connections to the science content they had been learning as well as raised new questions that tied to social justice and equity of access to clean water. In figure 7.2, the left-hand picture is of a school water fountain—a wonder when you ask yourself "What is in our water and where does it come from?" My answer is that it comes from water from streams and then goes through filters and purifiers to get rid of any diseases or germs. I took this picture because I wanted to show that every time we drink water, we need to think about all the stages it goes through. The right-hand picture in figure 7.2 is a running bathtub tap, which shows water we use to wash ourselves. But not all countries can wash themselves in clean water. Many countries in Africa have to get their water from underground with hand pumps or play pumps. Play pumps are easy to use, but hand pumps are much more difficult. And the water from these pumps can get dirty, so the people have to clean themselves with dirty water.

The final presentation was organized and rehearsed by the students. They selected the order of the pictures based on the different themes, and each student shared an abbreviated version of their larger narrative.

CONNECTING PHOTOVOICE TO LANGUAGE DEVELOPMENT OF EMERGING BILINGUALS

While this project wasn't directly working with emerging bilingual students, there are many opportunities for the methodology presented here to support the development of language acquisition and environmental literacy through photovoice. Academic language requires supports that aid in the learning of both language and content (Short & Echevarria, 2004); highlighted in this section are four components of photovoice that can benefit emerging bilinguals.

Small-Group Discussions

There are many advantages to using small-group discussions for emerging bilinguals. Teachers can determine how groups will be organized and can decide to organize around home-language groups or mixed-language groups. Small-group discussions of photos that students themselves took can bridge academic language with social or conversational language. Small groups can also provide the opportunity for students to do most the talking. In many

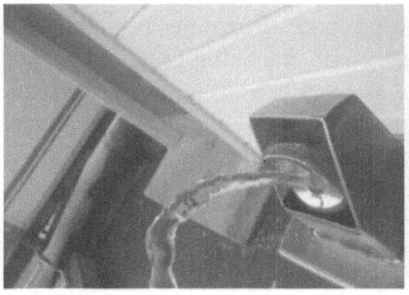 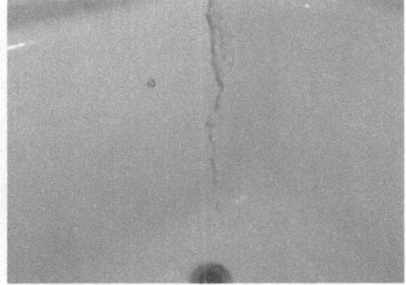

Figure 7.2. Photovoice image and transcription by students Alice and James

classrooms, teacher talk can reduce the opportunity students need to practice academic language. Small groups allow students to develop proficiency in language and use higher-level thinking and reasoning to interpret their photos.

Relevant Content That Can Build on Prior Knowledge

One of the most cited strategies to working with emerging bilinguals is to capitalize on their background and funds of knowledge. Funds of knowledge (Moll, Amanti, Neff, & Gonzalez, 1992) represent the home and community strengths and resources that students bring into the classroom. By tapping into students' funds of knowledge, teachers can use these as both a social and an intellectual resource, creating a meaning-centered model of learning in the classroom. Photovoice, by its very nature, is designed to privilege the voice and perspective of the individual taking the picture. As seen in the two student examples presented above, each connected their writing back to some aspect of their personal world (e.g., school, family, or neighborhood).

Providing opportunities for children to go into their own communities to take pictures creates relevant and authentic learning opportunities in which science content and language can be taught and assessed. Sharing photos and stories about one's life can also create valuable exchanges between teachers and students in which all are motivated to learn about one another, their families, cultures, and communities.

Building Oral Language, Writing, and Reading Comprehension

Photovoice has questions that are essential to generating critical dialogues. These questions act as conversation starters and can be modified into sentence prompts supporting emerging bilinguals in their writing. For example, the question "What do you see?" can be modified into a sentence starter: "In this picture I see . . ." The value of the sentence prompts is that they can be designed to focus on science content objectives as well as language objectives. The questions and prompts are also open ended with no right or wrong answer. They are specifically designed to promote classroom discourse and as such allow students to grapple with ideas while practicing English.

Once, short written pieces about images have been completed, students can practice reading comprehension through sharing individual narratives. The use of audio recorders can further support emerging bilinguals in both their listening and their writing skills as key ideas from conversations can be recalled and transcribed.

Use of Technology to Share Skills and Enhance Visual Literacy

The use of images allows for visual literacy development where images can provide scaffolds and context clues for students during discussions. Visual representations of science concepts that students have taken themselves can be more accessible for emerging bilinguals as they are sharing understandings in a nonlinguistic form. The use of technology can also provide an opportunity for students to support and teach one another. There is a lot of technical literacy involved in photovoice, and emerging bilinguals may possess these skills already, thus creating additional opportunities to develop oral language skills.

CONCLUSION

Photovoice, as presented here, provides a unique way to engage students with local, place-based issues that are relevant to their lives as well as the larger school and neighboring community. The use of technology (e.g., cameras and computers) creates an initial buy-in by students as they get excited to share both the cameras and their pictures with family and friends. For emerging bilinguals, photovoice provides a rich opportunity to connect classroom learning to students' lived experiences while supporting language learning and visual literacy. It also allows students to develop research and critical-thinking skills toward greater engagement in school and community life. Presenting photovoice for classroom practice as a series of stages allows for both adaptability and flexibility while still capturing the essence of the methodology: the voicing of children and youth experiences through critical dialogues of images.

REFERENCES

Bellino, M. E. (2015). Using photovoice as a critical youth participatory method in environmental education research. In K. Tobin & S. R. Steinberg (Eds.), *Doing educational research: A handbook* (2nd ed.; pp. 365–380). Bold visions in educational research 47. Rotterdam, Netherlands: SensePublishers.

Bellino, M. E., & Adams, J. D. (2014). Reimaging environmental education: Urban youths' perceptions and investigations of their communities. *Revista Brasileira de Pesquisa em Educação em Ciências, 14*(2), 27–38.

Berinstein, S., & Magalhaes, L. (2009). A study of the essence of play experience to children living in Zanzibar, Tanzania. *Occupational Therapy International, 16*(2), 89–106. doi:10.1002/oti.270.

Cahill, C. (2007). Doing research with young people: Participatory research and the rituals of collective work. *Children's Geographies, 5*(3), 297–312. doi:10.1080/14733280701445895.

Cammarota, J., & Fine, M. (2008). Youth participatory action research: A pedagogy for transformational resistance. In J. Cammarota & M. Fine (Eds.), *Revolutionizing education: Youth participatory action research in motion* (pp. 1–13). New York: Routledge.

Faircloth, S. C., Hynds, A., Jacob, H., Green, C., & Thompson, P. (2016). Ko wai au? Who am I? Examining the multiple identities of Māori youth. *International Journal of Qualitative Studies in Education, 29*(3), 359–380. doi:10.1080/09518398.2015.1053158.

Freire, P. (2000). *Pedagogy of the oppressed.* 30th anniversary ed. New York: Continuum.

Furman, G. C., & Gruenewald, D. A. (2004). Expanding the landscape of social justice: A critical ecological analysis. *Educational Administration Quarterly, 40*(1), 47–76.

Gonzalez, N., & Moll, L. C. (2002). Cruzando el puente: Building bridges to funds of knowledge. *Educational Policy, 16*(4), 623–641. doi:10.1177/0895904802016004009.

Gruenewald, D. A. (2003). The best of both worlds: A critical pedagogy of place. *Educational Researcher, 32*(4), 3–12.

Luttrell, W. (2010). "A camera is a big responsibility": A lens for analysing children's visual voices. *Visual Studies, 25*(3), 224–237.

Moll, L. C., Amanti, C., Neff, D., & Gonzalez, N. (1992). Funds of knowledge for teaching: Using a qualitative approach to connect homes and classrooms. *Theory into Practice, 31*(2), 132–141.

Nowell, B. L., Berkowitz, S. L., Deacon, Z., & Foster-Fishman, P. (2006). Revealing the cues within community places: Stories of identity, history, and possibility. *American Journal of Community Psychology, 37*(1–2), 63–76. doi:10.1007/s10464-005-9006-3.

Pritzker, S., LaChapelle, A., & Tatum, J. (2012). "We need their help": Encouraging and discouraging adolescent civic engagement through photovoice. *Children and Youth Services Review, 34*(11), 2247–2254. doi:10.1016/j.childyouth.2012.07.015.

Short, D., & Echevarria, J. (2004). Teacher skills to support English language learners. *Educational Leadership, 62*(4), 8–13.

Smith, D. E. (1987). *The everyday world as problematic: A feminist sociology.* Boston: Northeastern University Press.

Strack, R. W., Magill, C., & McDonagh, K. (2004). Engaging youth through photovoice. *Health Promotion Practice, 5*(1), 49–58. doi:10.1177/1524839903258015.

Wang, C. C. (1999). Photovoice: A participatory action research strategy applied to women's health. *Journal of Women's Health, 8*(2), 185–192.

———. (2006). Youth participation in photovoice as a strategy for community change. *Journal of Community Practice, 14*(1–2), 147–161. doi:10.1300/J125v14n01_09.

Wang, C. C., & Burris, M. A. (1997). Photovoice: Concept, methodology, and use for participatory needs assessment. *Health Education and Behavior, 24*(3), 369–387.

Wang, C. C., Cash, J. L., & Powers, L. S. (2000). Who knows the streets as well as the homeless? Promoting personal and community action through photovoice. *Health Promotion Practice, 1*(1), 81–89.

Wang, C. C., & Redwood-Jones, Y. A. (2001). Photovoice ethics: Perspectives from Flint photovoice. *Health Education and Behavior, 28*(5), 560–572. doi:10.1177/109019810102800504.

Chapter Eight

Exploring Identity through Image

E-Portfolios Supporting Cross-Curricular Learning for English Language Learners

Sarah Morrison

The context for this arts-based work is an independent secondary school located in Ontario, Canada. The student population of the school is culturally diverse with more than 200 international students from 35 nations with the entire student population at 750 students. The school offers an English-immersion and language-learning summer program for all international students who require this support before they begin school each fall. English language learner (ELL) students are often very engaged in the visual and performing arts program at the school, which offers courses in music, visual art, media arts, drama, and dance.

E-portfolios were introduced in the arts department more than 10 years ago and continue to be used, in some form, in all of the arts classes. E-portfolios are offered as authentic assessment tools engaging all learners in the exploration of their artistic identities using images as reflective artifacts. This chapter offers exemplars and excerpts to illustrate how e-portfolios have effectively supported ELL students, while also sharing templates and resources that can be used by teachers in e-portfolio integrations.

VIGNETTE: FINDING SUZY'S VOICE

Suzy always entered the music room with a smile but rarely spoke and hardly seemed to open her mouth when she was singing. Although she loved to sing and wanted to learn more about music, she was extremely nervous about singing and did not believe she had a singing voice. As anxious as she was about her singing voice, she was also very tentative about her spoken English skills as an English language learner and spoke as little as possible at the beginning of the year.

Throughout the year, Suzy slowly began to find her singing voice and became more confident within the class. One of the main class assessments was interactive e-portfolios that used photographs, video, and sound files to serve as the basis of individual and collaborative reflection. Suzy blossomed through the use of images to express her artistic thoughts. She participated actively in the e-portfolio work, which served to influence her class engagement and her overall self-assuredness.

Suzy also developed aspects of her artistic identity through her e-portfolio photographs and reflections. As her singing voice developed, her own voice as an artist emerged. In time, she became willing to engage in dialogue and share aspects of her story, of being a young person spending her first year in Canada, with her community of learners.

THEORETICAL BACKGROUND

There is a growing body of research on e-portfolios in arts education that can be connected to the development of English language learners. Portfolios or e-portfolios, the digital portfolio version, in the educational context are described as purposeful collections of student work that provide evidence of learning and exhibit a student's effort, progress, and achievement.

E-portfolios often include a wide range of material to demonstrate learning over a period of time in one or more curriculum areas (Rolheiser, Bower, & Stevahn, 2000). E-portfolio development has been linked to the facilitation of reflective practices and metacognition among students (Bauer & Dunn, 2003). The idea that reflection is a cognitive strategy that does not necessarily come easily to learners is supported by research in arts e-portfolio integration (Berg & Lind, 2003; Draves, 2009).

Additionally, certain technological advantages, such as the nonlinear nature of multimedia and the possibility of images, video, and audio clips being incorporated into e-portfolios, have been cited as particularly beneficial to learners in the arts context as well as to English language learners (Ancess & Darling-Hammond, 1994; Bingley, 1995).

Another area of arts education research is that of identity development in the student artist through e-portfolio learning (Morrison, 2004, 2010). In the past, arts educators have been critiqued for rarely engaging students in the types of creative activities and dialogues that contribute to the construction of their individualized artistic selves (Woodford, 1997). The development of identity and a sense of self as an artist are important processes for young people, with the goal of inspiring lifelong autonomous learning and enjoyment.

Further, as related to the context of this chapter, it is important to provide secondary school students with opportunities to reflect and shape their own artistic identities since they are at a key time in their lives as identity seekers (Jones & Perkins, 2006). Reflection has been credited as a means of fostering self-expression and artistic identity development (Reid, 2002). Reflections serve to encourage learners to see connections in their own work and to begin to view themselves in new roles, such as "musician" and "artist," leading to agency and further motivation for learning (Clark, 2010; Morrison, 2004, 2010; Rickards et al., 2008).

This research connects with the pedagogical approach of literacy through photography (LTP) that supports young people in exploring their world as they use photographs from their own lives as catalysts for written reflection and expression. LTP provides an opportunity for students to bring aspects of their informal artistic lives into the classroom and can serve to give both teachers a view into their students' lives and students a way to understand each other's diverse experiences. By incorporating student-selected photographs into e-portfolios assessments, teachers can begin to build shared understandings and collaborative learning communities in their classrooms.

PERFORMANCE-BASED ASSESSMENTS SUPPORTING ENGLISH LANGUAGE LEARNERS

Through performance-based assessments, the focus of the assessment shifts away from single skill learning to a more foundational view of process, understanding, and application (Mullen, Britten, & McFadden, 2005). This type of assessment also provides students with the opportunity to reflect on their learning and emphasizes the importance of the process as opposed to the final product as the goal.

Performance-based assessment is an effective means of providing encouragement as well as providing a model for continued learning. This form of assessment also works well because it takes into account the uniqueness of each learner, which can be an issue with other assessment forms such as standardized tests. E-portfolios can be classified as performance-based assessments and as such can support a large variety of learners including ELL students. All students, despite their differences in language skill, background, learning styles, and abilities, can create an e-portfolio within the set assessment structure.

Because e-portfolios emphasize the process of learning rather than a final product, there is increased time given for reflective thinking and analysis, and this increased reflection time can greatly benefit ELL students who cannot always form verbal or written thoughts as quickly as native English speakers.

E-PORTFOLIOS IN CROSS-CURRICULAR LEARNING

What might an e-portfolio look like in an arts classroom or as a cross-curricular project in multiple subject areas? E-portfolios can take on many different formats depending on their purpose. Many visual and performing artists collect artifacts of their creative works in tangible forms such as printed photographs, CD recordings, concert programs, or newspaper clippings. Others may choose to document their works through a digital collection saved in a variety of digital photos, video clips, and sound files.

These two examples can be thought of as a form of portfolio: the collection portfolio where one simply collects many artifacts about a person or a specific subject. The look and the type of e-portfolio can vary with the subject area or focus of the assessment. For example, a collection e-portfolio might be organized and saved to a personal cloud space, whereas an e-portfolio meant to share best works might be built using a social media platform or a more public space that can be promoted.

It is essential to consider these formatting choices when using e-portfolios with students in terms of online safety and how to best share the e-portfolio within a school community. There are many e-portfolio tools, including open-source technologies available to educators for free, and these can support e-portfolio creation in classroom settings while keeping student e-portfolios contained to a school-wide audience only.

As mentioned, the process-based portfolio is the recommended assessment tool format when working with ELL students in order to best support their reflective learning. This portfolio type is meant to show progress and development over a period of time and includes examples of best works as well as works in progress and artifacts that can represent struggles or challenges in the learning journey (Morrison, 2010).

These e-portfolios can be called "process folios" or growth portfolios as they include works in progress, best pieces, and significant pieces as determined by the student. This version of the e-portfolio also includes dates to monitor growth and uses criteria sets in relation to student goals and curriculum expectations as determined jointly by the student and the teacher. They are intended to show student progress in skill development and in understanding and applying content over a longer period of time.

It is important to note the significance of images, photographs, videos, and digital recordings as student-selected artifacts in these e-portfolios. This could be a monthly or bimonthly reflective process, depending on the length of the course or semester, where students select or create a digital artifact that represents an aspect of their learning. The students would then create a written or audio analysis reflecting on how this artifact, such as a meaningful photograph, reflects an aspect of their growth as a learner. For the ELL student, the use of images can provide an important role in expressing thoughts and ideas that they may not yet have the language capabilities to express in written format.

Through the use of images as reflective artifacts or images as prompts for a verbal reflection that could be recorded rather than written, ELL students are given another medium through which to communicate. It is important to remember that student voices can be expressed through various formats from written word to photograph, hand-drawn image, and a musical composition. While it is not always possible to allow for such variety in more traditional educational assessment tasks, such as an essay or multiple-choice test, these more abstract and nonwritten forms are often able to be incorporated effectively into e-portfolio work.

By the end of the school year, the students will have created a rich collection of artifacts and reflections through their e-portfolio work that document their development as learners. Alongside their primary role as educational assessment tools, the e-portfolios can become a source of pride for the students.

E-PORTFOLIO RESOURCES AND TEMPLATES

This section highlights key elements of e-portfolio integration that have been proven to work particularly well in arts curriculum contexts with a wide variety of learners, including ELL students, but that could be adapted for many different curriculum areas.

It is recommended to begin the e-portfolio introduction with an activity that focuses on sharing and introductions, such as a short biography using both words and images. This beginning task sets a professional tone because students begin to think of themselves as creative contributors as part of a larger community of learners, through both creating and sharing their own images and words as well as through reading the biographies of others. For ELL students, this biography task facilitates the sharing of their stories, including aspects of their cultural background they deem significant to communicate with the learning community.

Another consideration for teachers is the inclusion of self-assessment tasks before beginning the e-portfolio process. The self-assessment tasks can be designed to help the students develop realistic goals that they can revisit and reflect on throughout the year. Goal setting is an important part of the forethought or planning phase in self-regulated learning (SRL) theory that supports student engagement in their own learning processes (Zimmerman, 2000).

By using curriculum expectations as a guiding point to the development of these goals, the portfolio is connected to the course curriculum in a meaningful way. It can be valuable to allow the students to select the areas in which they wish to develop their goals, as opposed to imposing goals on them, in order to allow for agency and self-regulated learning skills to develop.

The use of a set structure for each e-portfolio entry works very well to give students a common framework through which to develop their ideas. The students have the element of choice in selecting their e-portfolio artifacts, which gives them ownership of the e-portfolio as well. Typically, in a process-folio format, the students choose what to include and what not to include in the e-portfolio, and this can be empowering to them as learners.

Here is an example of an e-portfolio monthly artifact reflection template for an arts e-portfolio:

Artifact Reflection Template

- Descriptive title
- Date of photograph or event
- Description of photograph or event
- Artistic analysis

Figures 8.1 through 8.3 show three examples of how the artifact reflection template might "look" in an actual e-portfolio.

The three monthly reflection exemplars demonstrate how a variety of artifacts can be used as the basis for reflective analysis of goals and artistic development. With a template, expectations can be set as to the information and analysis needed while also allowing for student choice in the actual artifacts as well as the design of the e-portfolio.

E-PORTFOLIO REFLECTION EXEMPLAR: "NOW I DARE TO SING OUT"

The following excerpt is an exemplar of an e-portfolio written reflection from an ELL student. This reflection came at the end of the school year, in June, when students were asked to look at their images and analysis from the year in their e-portfolios and reflect on their year and artistic growth overall. Suzy's reflection demonstrates her challenges and growth throughout the year culminating in her assertion that now she "dares to sing out"—a joyful point that she has come to in her personal artistic journey.

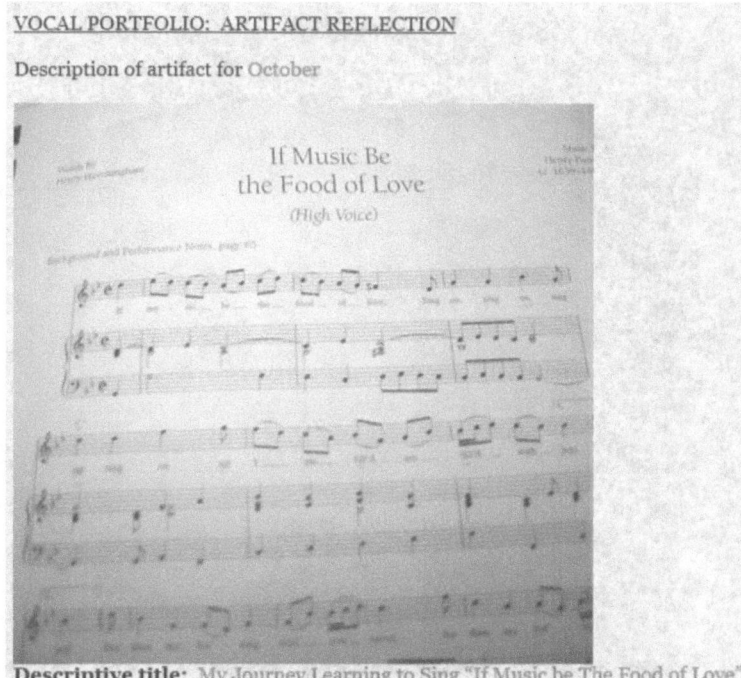

Figure 8.1.

Suzy's Reflection

My first year in the vocal class is amazing. We sing together, we worked together, and we have so much fun. At the beginning of the year, I am afraid of sing in front of people. I always feel that my voice is very strange and cannot find how to sing well. I know my singing skill is not very good, so I want to improve my singing skills. During this year, I had a lot of opportunity to performance and learn the strengths of others to sing. The most challenge for me is be relaxed sing in front of people, and that can make my voice being louder and let me be more confident. Now I dare to sing out.

ARTIFACT REFLECTION #1

Descriptive title: Rocking out!

Date of activity: September 15

Description of activity: Appleby Rocks is rock band comprised of singers and instrumentalist throughout the school. I was one of 4 singers in the band. We spent this rehearsal time creating harmonies by ear to popular songs.

Figure 8.2.

E-PORTFOLIO BIOGRAPHY EXEMPLAR: TOM

The following is an exemplar of an e-portfolio biography from a grade 10 ELL student named Tom. He effectively links experiences from his musical history and upbringing in Russia with his continued musical goals and development in Canada. Without the vocal biography portion of this assignment, Tom might not have shared these details of his musical story with others in the music classroom.

Tom's Reflection

Tom was born on July the 28th. He was born in Russia. He just came to Canada. His voice type is tenor. He studied the piano in Russia, he studied just for fun, actually he is not good at piano, but now he just takes part in

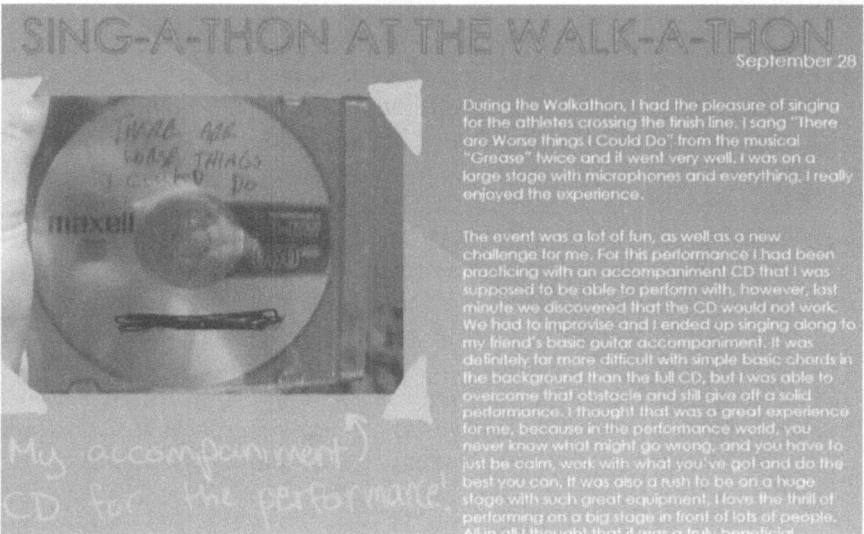

Figure 8.3.

Appleby of vocal class. He did not take part in some arts camp. But he had taken part in choirs in Russia. Tom performance in middle school a few times. He likes to sing together with others. But he was afraid when he was the only one to sing in front of many people. He is gradually tried to sing in front of many people. He would like to focus on singing this year. He likes singing, but his skill is not enough. Other interests outside of music is dance, Tom also likes dance. In this year, he will lay the foundation of singing.

Tom doesn't want to be a professional singer in the future. But he will still sing in the future, he will join more performance to improve herself. He likes play tennis very much. When he was grade 4, his mom has found a coach to him. He has got some prizes in Russia. He likes singing and sports very much.

THE E-PORTFOLIO DEVELOPMENT

Through the previous examples in this chapter, e-portfolios have been demonstrated to be empowering authentic assessment tools that can serve to support ELL student growth as well as support certain key skills such as self-regulated learning in all students.

Often it is helpful to have a few concise talking points when proposing a new implementation to administration. Here are eight key examples of how incorporating e-portfolios can support student learning, both for ELL students and for native English-speaking students.

1. E-portfolios can illustrate the process of learning over a period of time, rather than a single demonstration of learning at a fixed moment.
2. E-portfolios demonstrate student learning and achievement more accurately than do single test scores and, perhaps more importantly, can equip educators with more information on how to improve student learning.
3. E-portfolios are inclusive assessment tools allowing all students to demonstrate their learning in a variety of ways. Even ELL students at the beginning levels of English proficiency can engage in e-portfolio development.
4. E-portfolios encourage more authentic and "real-life" learning opportunities by encouraging students to connect images and artifacts from their informal (non-school) learning to their formal (classroom) education.
5. E-portfolios can instill a sense of pride and agency in learners by providing them with evidence of their development over time.
6. E-portfolios can help to develop self-analysis and self-regulated learning skills in students by allowing them to connect their development to specific learning goals.
7. E-portfolios can help schools create a shared vision for student learning, aligned to standards. This can be particularly important when assessing ELL students, in that teachers can look beyond language errors and focus on how well students demonstrate an understanding of concepts or express their ideas.
8. E-portfolios can accommodate choice in the format of student expression through written word, images, or digital recordings, allowing for students to share their learning in a variety of ways. Additionally, due to the process-focused nature of e-portfolios, there is increased time for reflective thinking skills to develop that can be particularly beneficial to ELL students who may be struggling to think and communicate quickly in a new language.

As education moves toward project-based learning and the integration of 21st-century learning and technology skills for K–12 programs, e-portfolios become increasingly relevant as powerful assessment tools for students. It is very much worth the planning time that it takes to design and implement e-portfolios as authentic assessment tools in the classroom.

E-PORTFOLIO RESOURCES FOR TEACHERS

There are numerous e-portfolio platforms available to teachers, and these technology tools are being changed and improved constantly. Many valuable resources can be found through simple online searches, including searching university programs with comprehensive e-portfolio guides. This e-portfolio resource list includes a variety of open-source, digital portfolio platforms and tutorials where students can create personal e-portfolios.

- http://www.wikispaces.com
- https://www.foliospaces.org
- https://edublogs.org
- https://wordpress.com
- https://pathbrite.com
- https://www.portfoliogen.com

It is important to remember that e-portfolios can also be created using a variety of different platforms from Google Sites to social media platforms and Word documents with embedded photographs. There is really no single correct way of designing and integrating e-portfolios into K–12 classrooms, and often the students can be helpful in offering ideas and co-designing the e-portfolio formats.

E-PORTFOLIO DESIGN QUESTIONS

As previously outlined, there are several different types, formats, and templates for e-portfolio assessment tools that can be incorporated into classrooms of all levels. It is up to the individual teacher or team of educators to choose the most appropriate e-portfolio design and focus for their students, keeping in mind that e-portfolios can be altered and adapted to best suit the learning goals.

As teachers consider implementing e-portfolios in their classrooms, here are a few questions to think about in this regard:

- What are your pedagogical goals in using this assessment tool?
- What will the e-portfolio look like? What form will it take?
- How will images and other multimedia forms, such as digital recordings, be included in the e-portfolio?
- Who will select the contents of the e-portfolio?
- When and how will the e-portfolio be reviewed?
- How can the e-portfolio be shared among the class to create a community of learners?

The e-portfolio tool can be a valuable tool for all ELL students in supporting their learning goals and allowing them to express themselves through a combination of words and images. Educators can continue to empower students by recognizing the diversity in the classroom and giving each individual student choices in how to best express themselves throughout their learning journeys.

REFERENCES

Ancess, J., & Darling-Hammond, L. (1994). *Authentic teaching, learning, and assessment with new English learners at International High School: A series on authentic assessment and accountability.* New York: Columbia University Teachers College, National Center for Restructuring Education, Schools and Teaching.

Bauer, W., & Dunn, R. (2003). The electronic portfolio in music teacher education. *Journal of Music Teacher Education, 13*(1), 7–20.

Berg, M., & Lind, V. (2003). Preservice music teacher electronic portfolios: Integrating reflection and technology. *Journal of Music Teacher Education, 12*(2), 18–28.

Bingley, A. (1995, Winter). Portfolios in a second language: ESL students share learning with the English-speaking community. *Portfolio News, 6*(2), 1, 12–13.

Clark, J. (2010). The digital imperative: Making the case for a 21st-century pedagogy. *Computers and Composition, 27*(1), 27–35.

Draves, T. (2009). Portfolio assessment in student teaching: A reliability study. *Journal of Music Teacher Education, 19*(1), 25–38.

Holm, G. (2014). Photography as a research method. In P. Leavy (Ed.), *The Oxford handbook of qualitative research* (pp. 380–402). New York: Oxford University Press.

Jones, K. R., & Perkins, D. F. (2006). Youth and adult perceptions of their relationships within community-based youth programs. *Youth and Society, 38*(1), 90–109.

Morrison, S. (2004). Bringing a world of choral music into the classroom (and assessing it!). *Canadian Music Educator, 46*(2), 34–35.

———. (2010). Sure, I'm a singer! The empowering effect of vocal portfolios at the secondary school level. In K. Adams & T. Reynish (Eds.), *Sharing the voices: The phenomenon of singing international symposium V* (pp. 240–248). St. John's, Newfoundland: Faculty of Education, Memorial University of Newfoundland.

Mullen, L., Britten, J., & McFadden, J. (2005). *Digital portfolios in teacher education.* Indianapolis, IN: JIST Works.

Reid, S. (2002). Creativity: A fundamental need of adolescent learners. In T. Sullivan & L. Willingham (Eds.), *Creativity and music education* (Vol. 1, pp. 100–109). Toronto, ON: Canadian Music Educators' Association.

Rickards, W., Diez, M., Ehley, L., Guilbault, L., Loacker, G., Hart, J., & Smith, P. (2008). Learning, reflection, and electronic portfolios: Stepping toward an assessment practice. *Journal of General Education, 57*(1), 31–50.

Rolheiser, C., Bower, B., & Stevahn, L. (2000). *The portfolio organizer.* Reston, VA: Association for Supervision and Curriculum Development.

Woodford, P. (1997). Music education, culture, and democracy: Sociality and individuality. *Canadian Music Educator, 39*(1), 15–18.

Zimmerman, B. J. (2000). Attainment of self-regulation: A social cognitive perspective. In M. Boekaerts, P. Pintrich, & M. Zeidner (Eds.), *Self-regulation: Theory, research, and applications* (pp. 13–39). Orlando, FL: Academic Press.

Chapter Nine

The Selfie Project

Using Photographs to Improve Writing with Diverse Learners

Browning Neddeau

> The selfies transported me from the mountaintop to the ground level, which provided me with a much better view of the details.—student

A drunken gaffe that resulted in a trip and subsequent cut lip was the first documented selfie back in 2002. There remains, however, disagreement as to whether the drunken Australian man was the first documented selfie case. It was not until 2013 that *selfie* was nominated as a Word of the Year (Zimmer, Solomon, & Carson, 2014). In addition to its inherent self-promotion aspect, the selfie has been used to teach art (McMeans, 2015), write soliloquies (Plumb, 2014), and promote classroom discussion (Romano, 2014).

Selfie research and pedagogy that uses selfies to teach concepts is a growing field with international appeal. Searching for the term *selfie* on a scholarly database, when the search is limited to scholarly, peer-reviewed journals and the specific discipline of education, returns only six results related to the current study on using selfies as a pedagogical tool. None of the research reviewed, however, explored the use of selfies either in comic strips or as a vehicle to aid in the writing process.

The Selfie Researchers Network (2016) is an international organization interested in the social and cultural effects of selfies and includes a budding list of selfie scholarship. As the interest and use of selfies continue to grow in our 21st-century classrooms, exploring ways to build upon the selfie across the curriculum in reaching diverse learners with varying English-language-proficiency skills is timely and necessary.

The creation of this arts-based lesson was in a K–6 urban public school in San Jose, California. The school was situated in the most economically disadvantaged neighborhood in San Jose and served approximately 480 students where 96 percent of the students qualified for free or reduced lunch. Of those students, 72 percent were English language learners with the majority of students speaking either Spanish or Vietnamese as their primary language.

The Selfie Project, in its fourth-grade context, was used as an example for undergraduate students conducting an in-depth investigation of creating stories using selfies in comic-strip form to tell the story of a place, demonstrating the broad potential applications for this work in terms of age/grade level of students.

In general, students at the school performed poorly on standardized assessments in writing. In a fourth-grade classroom at this school site, the Selfie Project was developed to best meet the diverse language learning needs of the students. Since its initial development, data is continually collected from students enrolled in an undergraduate, general-education course where 33 percent of its students come from communities similar to the initial population where English is not the primary home language.

This chapter explores a lesson exemplar on how the Selfie Project unfolded in a classroom to effectively support English learners. Suggestions on ways educators can incorporate the Selfie Project across the curriculum to support student success are addressed.

VIGNETTE: LEARNING FROM THE CLASSROOM LIBRARY

The fourth-grade classroom contained a collection of perceived high-interest books at different reading levels. There was a variety of reading options including chapter books, picture books, fiction, and nonfiction. Students had choices to consider when visiting the classroom library.

The ongoing challenge was to advance the students' reading proficiency with self-selected reading materials that interested them. It was not uncommon to observe students who struggled to read either hide behind thick chapter books with the occasional flipping of the page to give the illusion of reading or select a nonfiction picture book of which they could visually capture the main ideas.

One section of the classroom library, however, was so popular that books would not stay on the shelf long enough to collect dust: the graphic novels. The collection of graphic novels included classic books presented in a comic-book form. Students from a wide range of English proficiency enjoyed the graphic novels. The high interest led to lessons structured as comic strips. Each frame in the comic strip was described as a photograph. The Selfie

Project lesson emerged from the ongoing student interest and understanding of comic books.

THEORETICAL FRAMEWORK

The use of images to reach and teach English learners is well documented (Cecil, 2011). Jatila van der Veen (2012) suggested that images, specifically drawing, help students connect their "inner language" (p. 365) with experiences through a visual representation. Scott McCloud's (1993, 2006) works in comics provide the study's theoretical underpinning, specifically the role of word/picture combinations. McCloud (1993, 2006) identifies seven categories of word/picture combinations that are emphasized in the Selfie Project. Two of the emphasized word/picture combinations occurred at different parts of the Selfie Project: picture-specific and intersecting.

Students used the picture-specific combination where the picture provided all the necessary information to the reader. The collection of photographs (selfies) told a story without the students using words or text to elaborate on the story. In an elementary classroom with a high number of English learners, illustrations with a sequence of events provided a foundation for building language skills.

In a comic strip, for example, there may be two panels. Imagine that the first panel shows a character sitting in front of a large bowl of spaghetti. The character is shown wearing a bib and holding a giant fork. In the second panel, the character's face is covered in what appears to be spaghetti sauce and the large bowl that once held spaghetti is now an empty bowl. The reader can create a story from these two panels.

However, there may also be a story that happens between the panels that can lead to further discussion. In other words, the arrangement of the panels guides the reader in gaining a sense of time in the sequence (e.g., the character sits in front of a bowl of spaghetti; then the character sits in front of an empty bowl that was once filled with spaghetti). The reader infers and understands that time has elapsed between panels one and two.

In addition to the picture-specific combination, students used intersecting (McCloud, 2006) at a later stage in the Selfie Project. Intersecting suggests that both the words and the pictures work together, but each part also provides information independent of the other. The use of comics in reaching and teaching English learners bridges the available literature on the use of images in teaching English learners with a variety of word/picture combinations.

IMPLEMENTING THE SELFIE PROJECT: A LESSON EXEMPLAR

Selfies seem to be a ubiquitous phenomenon that captures the essence of the comic book fascination through photography. The following is an example of how the Selfie Project was implemented in a writing project centered on the topic of community. This section first establishes the context of the lesson exemplar.

The lesson exemplar used data collected at a public university during the 2015–2016 academic year in an undergraduate, general-education course. The university is situated in a rural community where 56 percent of the students are the first generation in their family to attend college. Although the data collection is ongoing, this chapter shares the lesson exemplar in regard to a sense of self-awareness in writers. Students participated in the lesson as part of a course exemplar for integrating technology into the classroom through use of a class website. Although all students in the class spoke and wrote in English, some students were multilingual.

The Selfie Project relied on students to use their personal electronic devices, primarily cellular telephones, to complete the photography portion. With the abundance of cellular telephones with cameras in classrooms, most students had access to some sort of portable electronic device to participate in the Selfie Project. Students who did not have access to a portable electronic device were offered the use of one. The majority of students used their personal laptops for the writing portions of the Selfie Project.

The Selfie Project included nine steps that are outlined in table 9.1. The final step of the project is a reflective writing assignment for students to note any observations from their writing experience, which was used for this chapter. In its present form, the Selfie Project has been used for students to write about their community.

As indicated in table 9.1, the Selfie Project took place over two class sessions (day 1 and day 2). First, students received a handout with a list of eight clues. The clues were riddles to places around the university community. The handout of clues was discussed as a scavenger hunt to the students. One example of a clue: "I am pretty busy up to three times per day (around the same times, too)." The answer to this particular clue was the dining commons, which is the university's cafeteria.

For step 2, students were given approximately one hour and twenty minutes to search the university campus and take a selfie with their answer to each clue. The university sits on a large piece of land, and the answers to the clues were located throughout the university's campus. Therefore, an hour and twenty minutes provided a reasonable amount of time to locate answers.

Next, the class reconvened and discussed their answers to the riddles. Selfies were not shared at this time, but students shared their answers in a

Table 9.1. Steps of the Selfie Project implementation over a two-day period

Step	Description
	Day 1
1	Receives a handout with a list of clues
2	Takes a selfie with their answer to each clue
3	As a whole group, discusses answers to the clues
	Day 2
4	Writes a story about their community (e.g., university campus) *without* using selfies
5	Writes a story about their community (e.g., university campus) *using* the selfies
6	Rereads their story *and* reviews their selfies about their community and adds details from their selfies into the story
7	Rereads their story once more for any final edits
8	Writes and publishes final draft of story
9	Writes a reflection on the experience

whole-class discussion. If students had answers outside of the original intent of the clue, then they were given time to explain them.

For the next class session, step 4 (day 2), students arrived to class and typed a story about the university's campus community *without* using their selfies. Students were given approximately 20 minutes to write their story. The following six areas of writing were illuminated on the projector screen for students to "think about the following items in your story": sequencing, descriptive words and details, transitional words, narrator, beginning, and conclusion. These six areas were not discussed at this time of the lesson. Students posted their stories to a classroom website.

Next, students wrote a story (on binder paper) about their university's campus community *using* the selfies. Although the plan provided students approximately 20 minutes to write their stories, most students completed their story in about 16 minutes. Students were instructed to use at least four of their eight selfies in their story. Again, students were asked to think about sequencing, descriptive words and details, transitional words, narrator, beginning, and conclusion.

In step 6, all the students reread their stories that used the selfies and reviewed their selfies. From their rereading and review of selfies, students were asked to consider adding details from their selfies into the story. No additional instructions were given at this time about what details to consider.

After each student reread his or her story for any final edits (step 7), they typed out their final draft (step 8). The students posted their final story to the classroom website. Students were able to read each other's final stories on the classroom website, if desired.

Lastly, students typed out a reflection on the Selfie Project experience (step 9). The educator used the final reflections to explore to what extent the selfies created a sense of self-awareness in their writing.

SELFIE LESSON EXEMPLAR OUTCOMES

The purpose of the Selfie Project was to examine to what extent selfies create a sense of self-awareness in writers. Table 9.2 indicates words that emerged in the student reflections that relate to a self-awareness in writing. As table 9.2 illustrates, the words that emerged in both fall 2015 and spring 2016 are connected to specific aspects of writing such as descriptive words and sequencing.

One student's reflection captured the concepts shared across multiple student reflections of details and recall, as it related to using the selfies in the writing. "The selfies helped me tell the story about our campus by giving me details of specific places. I was able to be more descriptive about our campus community because I had pictures of the places I wrote about. Without the pictures, I would not have been able to recall as much detail about the places around campus."

Another student's comment referred to the story line without using the keyword of *story line*, as tabulated in table 9.2. The student stated that the details observed in the selfies helped the student develop the plot and it gave "details for the reader visually on where the story is taking place." Other students reported that the selfies helped them create a story they felt the reader could follow.

Flow and recall (i.e., remembering) emerged as themes across student reflections that seemed related to story line; however, the researcher ascertained that flow and recall were not synonymous with story line across student reflections and, therefore, should be reported separately.

Table 9.2. Words that emerged in reflective writings, fall 2015 frequency, spring 2016 frequency, and writing connections

Word	Fall 2015 frequency	Spring 2016 frequency	Writing connection
Detail or details	10	7	descriptive words
Storyline or story line	1	3	sequencing
Flow	1	2	sequencing
Remember or recall	6	5	sequencing

Flow and recall were themes that were mentioned explicitly in the student reflections multiple times in both the fall 2015 and the spring 2016 terms. Table 9.2, however, does not capture the various other occurrences of concepts of flow and recall in the student reflections. For example, one student wrote that the selfies "provided a nice layout for my story." Another student stated that the selfies "gave me an outline of some sort to help me come up with a story that I felt was good." Both of these examples are absent of the word flow but suggest that words like *layout* and *outline* attempt to describe flow.

Selfies used in the Selfie Project suggested that students took different approaches to the actual selfie-taking task. Some students, for instance, made certain poses or facial expressions in their selfies. Other students made a variety of facial expression across all of their selfies. In the Selfie Project lesson exemplar, there was not a specific connection explored between the variety of facial expressions in any particular student's selfies and the subsequent writing.

The students reported that the Selfie Project increased their awareness in their writing and acted as visual cues for developing their stories. Students reported the selfies helped with story sequence, use of appropriate adjectives, details, and transitional words when writing a piece. The Selfie Project writings also provided additional insights into how selfies can help all writers, especially English learners.

SELFIES AS A STRATEGY TO LEARN

The lesson exemplar detailed in this chapter can act as a guide for one possible way to integrate selfies in the classroom. Embedding strategy instruction (Meltzer, Sales Pollica, & Barzillai, 2007), like the use of comics in writing instruction, is a field-tested practice with promising results with diverse learners. The Selfie Project's reflective narratives indicated that students' use of selfies heightened their sense of self-awareness in regard to the planning, organization, and recall for the writing.

The lesson exemplar's outcome indicated selfies assist students in identifying a sequence and flow in their writing. Furthermore, the selfies guided writers in building awareness to the role of details in their writing. These aspects of writing are relevant especially as educators explore the content of student stories and consider other ways to incorporate selfies across the curriculum.

SUGGESTIONS FOR INCORPORATING SELFIES ACROSS THE CURRICULUM FOR STUDENT SUCCESS

Educators may find the Selfie Project a useful idea to incorporate into the curriculum to support student success. While schools implement 1:1 tablet or laptop programs (Johnson, Adams Becker, Estrada, & Freeman, 2015), the need to physically engage students in their learning is omnipresent. Also, schools across the United States are adopting the Common Core State Standards (CCSS; National Governors Association Center for Best Practices & Council of Chief State School Officers, 2010) and the four Cs of CCSS: communication, collaboration, critical thinking, and creativity (National Education Association, n.d.). Below are some ideas to consider on how to integrate the Selfie Project into a wide range of curricular studies.

Curriculum Review

Students could use selfies to document evidence of their learning throughout a unit of study. At the end of the unit, students could revisit their selfies to reflect and write about their learning throughout the unit. An educator may consider different options to store and access the selfies for the curriculum review. The educator may create a technology center in the classroom where each student has an electronic folder to store their selfies, a folder on a tablet, or a flash drive with the selfies.

Oral Presentations

Selfies can support students during an oral presentation. The educator could have students display a selfie or a sequence of selfies that help guide the presentation. Students can use the details in the selfie or selfies and provide talking points in the presentation.

Genres of Writing

Selfies are a novel and engaging way to teach genres of writing and support student success in structured writing (e.g., topic sentence, evidences, and conclusion). In opinion writing, for instance, students can use selfies that help them write about their perspective on a topic. Organizing selfies around a topic or theme permits students to develop an argument grounded in evidence. Selfies are helpful in narrative writing because students may struggle with identifying a narrator or characters in a story. The selfies allow the student to be the narrator of the story.

FINAL THOUGHTS

Writing in English can be a daunting and arduous task for students, especially if English is not their first language. McCloud's work (1993, 2006) provides a framework for understanding how visuals reach across language barriers and build steps in the writing process that scaffolds students in developing as writers in English. Although this chapter focused on students' self-awareness in their writing, it also opened a window into understanding the power of visuals in communicating ideas regardless of English language proficiency and how an arts-based approach to writing instruction can provide promising results for English learners.

REFERENCES

Cecil, N. (2011). *Striking a balance: A comprehensive approach to early literacy.* Scottsdale, AZ: Holcomb Hathaway.
Johnson, L., Adams Becker, S., Estrada, V., & Freeman, A. (2015). *NMC horizon report: 2015 K–12 edition.* Austin, TX: New Media Consortium.
McCloud, S. (1993). *Understanding comics: The invisible art.* New York: William Morrow.
———. (2006). *Making comics: Storytelling secrets of comics, manga and graphic novels.* New York: HarperCollins.
McMeans, A. (2015). Incorporating social media in the classroom. *Education, 135*(3), 289–290.
Meltzer, L., Sales Pollica, L., & Barzillai, M. (2007). Executive function in the classroom: Embedding strategy instruction into daily teaching practices. In L. Meltzer (Ed.), *Executive function in education: From theory to practice* (pp. 165–194). New York: Guilford.
National Education Association. (n.d.). *Preparing 21st-century students for a global society: An educator's guide to the "four Cs."* Retrieved from http://www.nea.org.
National Governors Association Center for Best Practices & Council of Chief State School Officers. (2010). *Common core state standards for English language arts and literacy in history/social studies, science, and technical subjects.* Washington, DC: Authors.
Plumb, J. (2013–2014). News, fiction and humour from the world of education. *ATA* [Alberta Teachers' Association] *News, 48*(15), 12.
Romano, M. (2014). Putting the science into science teacher. *Science Teacher, 81*(7), 12.
Selfie Researchers Network. (2016). Scholars studying selfies. Retrieved from http://www.selfieresearchers.com.
van der Veen, J. (2012). Draw your physics homework? Art as a path to understanding in physics teaching. *American Educational Research Journal, 49*(2), 356–407.
Zimmer, B., Solomon, J., & Carson, C. E. (2014). Among the new words. *American Speech, 89*(2), 190–207. doi:10.1215/00031283-2772068.

Chapter Ten

Who Are You? I Am...

Activist Art to Author ELL Identities

Sheron L. Mark

Identification as an English language learner, or ELL, is more than a description of one's proficiency with the English language; it is a historical sociopolitical status intricately connected with educational, socioeconomic, and cultural marginalization in U.S. society.

ELLs have been regularly labeled as failing, deviant, or culturally deficient, and these shortcomings are often blamed on their home communities (Nieto & Bode, 2012). ELLs are vulnerable to being systematically tracked into lower academic coursework and instruction focused on developing English language proficiency as opposed to college preparation coursework, and this occurs despite ELLs' variable levels of academic preparation for advanced coursework (Kanno & Kangas, 2014). There have been minimal expectations of postsecondary education and professional career involvement for ELLs (Callahan & Gándara, 2004).

Correspondingly, ELLs have been overrepresented in low-wage, service-sector jobs and economic systems (Moran & Petsod, 2003). Worse, institutional policies sustain, rather than disrupt, the association between ELLs and low-level work (Jefferies, 2014; Warriner, 2007).

In schools, ELLs' languages and cultures are cast out in the forms of ruling out or limiting bi-/multilingual education (Johnson & Fine, 2016; Ulanoff & Vega-Castaneda, 2003). Rather, in place of bi-/multilingual education, ELLs are confronted with widespread messages that present English proficiency as the necessary first step to mainstream educational engagement and high-quality learning (Callahan, 2005) and as the gateway to economic self-sufficiency and high-quality lives (Warriner, 2007). This has the effect of diminishing their native languages and cultures and of positioning English as superior.

Powerful individual and institutional forces function to categorize and essentialize highly diverse ELL populations into a few rigid identities within our complex, diverse, and ever-changing society (Harklau, 2000). As a result, an ELL identifier has the impact of overshadowing the other competencies, literacies, and aspects of culture among these populations. More than overlooking the skills and resources among ELLs, character-based assumptions tend to be made about the population, including their moral and legal standing, their work ethic and determination, and how deserving they are of the "American dream" (Jefferies, 2008).

Ultimately, oppressive ideologies and institutional barriers limit ELLs' opportunity to learn and limit their postsecondary and professional career prospects. Even more, these contribute to the perceived identities of ELLs, as well as the ongoing acceptance and treatment of ELLs and immigrant populations in the United States. As such, ELLs must be supported in authoring their own diverse, multifaceted, complex, and uniquely hybrid identities. ELLs must be supported in being able to voice for themselves who they are and what they need to succeed.

ACTIVISM THROUGH THE CREATIVE ARTS

In order to challenge the oppressive ideologies and institutional barriers that influence the school experiences of ELL youth, this classroom-based project focused on youth's engagement with the creative arts as a means to social critique and activism. Activism in art education is defined as "a variety of work toward social and political consciousness, empowerment, and change . . . not one of indoctrination or the masses being led by the few. . . . Instead, activism focuses on building a [critical] democracy (Giroux, 1995)" (Campana, 2011, p. 281).

Art has a rich activist tradition. Rather than as isolated creators, some artists see their work as connected to real-world issues and as means to advance social justice and positive change (Campana, 2011). Through their engagement with and production of art, this activist connection can be extended to youth.

Art facilitates experiences in support of developing a productive activist stance for social change, including growth in knowledge of self, exploration of issues and themes relevant to the community of artists, exposure to and interactions with others different from oneself, deconstructing and reconstructing culture, and more (Gude, 2007).

Even more, contrary to the commonplace assumption that youth are "apathetic," youth do express interest in and perspectives on sociopolitical issues in diverse ways and spaces (Akom, Cammarota, & Ginwright, 2008; Solorzano & Delgado Bernal, 2001), including "informal, individualized and everyday activities" such as art and music (Harris, 2010, p. 9).

MEETING THE NEEDS OF YOUTH THROUGH ACTIVIST ART AND CRITICAL PEDAGOGY OF PLACE

This activist art classroom project took place within a large, metropolitan high school (total enrollment = 1,423 in 2015–2016) within a U.S. midwestern/southern public school district. The high school population was highly socioculturally diverse, composed of 42.5 percent black, 38.1 percent white (not Hispanic), 14 percent Latino, 5.4 percent other racial and ethnic identities, and 71.9 percent participation in the free or reduced lunch program in 2015–2016.

There was a high ELL population (7.5 percent at the school compared to 5.3 percent throughout the entire school district). Students identified as having limited English proficiency was 9.3 percent (which included ELLs) and was also higher than the district-wide level of 6.6 percent in 2015–2016. Linguistic diversity was very high throughout the public school district. From data retrieved from the 2014–2015 and 2015–2016 public school district accountability reports, more than 109 languages were represented throughout this urban school district.

Engagement in activist art was believed to be particularly relevant for ELL youth at this particular school and in this city, as well as students of color, low-income youth, and English-speaking immigrant youth, as these nondominant students have long experienced significant social challenges in and beyond the classroom, including persistently low educational achievement, poverty, homelessness, joblessness, violent crime, health challenges, and more.

The activist art project would entail the youth learning about and responding to oppression based on their lived experiences. This was reflective of a critical pedagogy of place (Gruenewald, 2003), which centers on teaching and learning to support youth in naming, critiquing, and responding to power in society that influences their lives. This includes the ideologies and policies that shape the sociopolitical definition of an ELL described earlier.

Importantly, in response to the named oppression, a critical pedagogy of place also emphasizes that youth take action to advance equity and support real change in their lives and for others. In the project, this action would be potentially enacted through provoking critical conversations centered on their creative artwork.

The activist art project was not designed exclusively for ELLs and thus engaged all members of the learning environment—ELLs and monolingual

English-speaking students and teachers. As a result, all students would participate in the work of critical pedagogy of place (Gruenewald, 2003) and responding actively to oppression. Ultimately, through this activist art project, all students and educators may potentially develop greater levels of understanding of ELL populations and greater abilities to critique and reform institutional barriers to ELLs' educational and life success.

The vignettes in this chapter center on the findings for select ELL students in the project. The desired outcomes for all youth through this project were as follows: (1) to enhance classroom-based experiences such that the experiences and strengths of the students, as opposed to their failures, were recognized centrally in the learning environment; (2) to strengthen feelings of social connectedness and belonging to their school community through teaching and learning directly related to their lived experiences; and (3) to increase understanding of the cultures students bring to school through student-driven creative art.

OVERVIEW OF ACTIVIST ART CLASSROOM PROJECT

Two white, female, English-speaking, American art teachers collaborated with a local creative and performing arts institution to implement the classroom-based activist art project. Project leaders from the arts institution included a white male and a white female, both English speaking. I, a black, female, English-speaking Trinidadian native, participated in the project through an ongoing partnership between my university and the public school.

The activist art project involved the youth learning about a historical genocide of a population in Europe and responding to the oppression through creative arts. For the project, the students attended a play focused on the genocide, as well as the stories of several people from the population. Beyond the play, they continued to learn from survivors who detailed their experiences in a documentary. They also learned from firsthand conversations with one descendent of survivors.

Following this experience, several class sessions were focused on establishing community and trust amongst the youth, teachers, and project leaders such that they could "react" openly and explore oppression in their lives. The youth then transitioned into their creative arts process in which they collectively developed a response to the oppression and produced artwork to communicate their argument. The activist art production could have been of any tradition from visual to performing. The students decided on a mural (figure 10.1) in which they celebrated their differences yet united in resistance to inequity.

In the mural, they showcased the diverse and myriad aspects of themselves in the form of "I am . . ." statements. Students completed the statement

"I am . . ." with something personal and collected statements from school community members—that is, students, teachers, and staff members. Each "I am . . ." statement was written on a colored adhesive note, and collectively these formed the multicolored background of the mural. A large three-dimensional structure of lips was then placed atop the "I am . . ." statements with "Stand Out Together" painted on them.

The argument made through the activist art was that (1) they were all different; (2) they should be different; (3) they can be united without sacrificing that difference or the strength of their union; and (4) their stance was one against physical, verbal, or symbolic violence, for example, in the form of xenophobia, racism, sexism, or homophobia—even if the violence was not directed toward them individually.

"I AM . . .": DEVELOPMENTAL GAINS FOR ELLS THROUGH ACTIVIST ART

To investigate the impact of the activist art project on participating ELL students, I focused on four ELL youth who were interviewed prior to and following the project. Qualitative findings are presented next.

First, the design of the instructional unit was such that the experiences, strengths, and resources of ELLs were central as instructional resources for

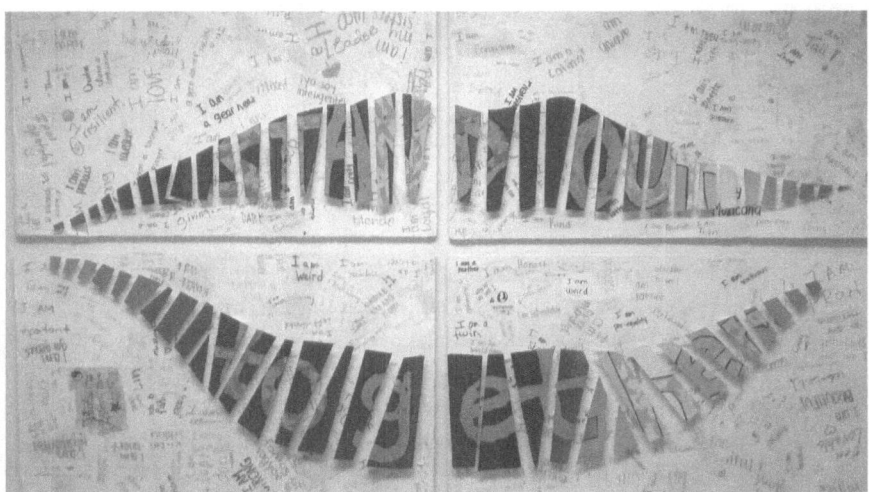

Figure 10.1. *Stand Out Together*, an activist art mural created by Seneca High School art students and their teachers, Mrs. Melissa Molohon and Mrs. Kelly Thompson, on speaking out about diversity in a changing world.

the learning process for all students, including ELLs themselves. Specifically, the mural contained hundreds of "I am . . ." statements, which captured core aspects of the identities of the students of these two art classes, their art teachers, and students, teachers, and staff and community members beyond the art classes.

The "I am . . ." statements were essential instructional resources in the art-activism project. Class-based discussions in the creation of the statements, the collection of school-wide statements, and the eventual showcasing of the statements in the final art show were all critically educational as they communicated the vast diversity of identities in the school and what each person saw as important about themselves.

The ELL youth of focus shared who they were including beyond their English-proficiency status. For instance, Dahlia, a female, junior, Spanish-English bilingual, shared "real" aspects of her identity: "I am from Mexico. . . . I am a Catholic. . . . I brought some of that from home to bring out the real me . . . for this project" (April 2016).

This instructional practice and the symbolism of the artwork was a strong communication of pushing beyond traditional boundaries of labeling people in predetermined categories, including being English-proficient. Dahlia was supported in writing about her identity as an ELL, which served as an important educational opportunity for the creators and viewers of the artwork.

The learning was bidirectional with ELLs teaching others about the complexity of identity and culture, while learning about other students as well. Tomás, a Cuban native and a Spanish-English bilingual, discussed learning about the culture of his ELL classmate, Hawa, who was from Iraq but was forced to relocate with her family to Egypt due to war. Tomás learned from Hawa's stories, saying, "I was in a group with [Hawa]. . . . We learned . . . about her. She told us about her family, what she does . . . at home, about her culture" (April 2016).

Second, the ELL students displayed an enhanced understanding and perspective of diversity as a result of producing and assembling the "I am . . ." statements. For instance, the "I am . . ." statements functioned to allow Dahlia to showcase her ELL culture in a more complex way, beyond simply her English language proficiency. Dahlia taught her classmates, teachers, school community, and more about her "real" ELL identity, which included being a Mexican Catholic. She added an individual, a historical, and a more complex perspective to her place as an ELL in her school community, which may serve to encourage ongoing dialogue.

Additionally, the ELL youth indicated that they had developed positive perspectives on diversity from the art production experience. These positive perspectives are important in developing resilient attitudes to the oppressive and marginalizing societal forces experienced by ELLs in the United States. Dahlia said, "I think that people will hear and listen to how we are all different and people will want to explain . . . do that themselves . . . because we showed who we are . . . [and] we're gonna ask the question: Who are you?" (April 2016).

"Who are you?" according to Dahlia, was a positive and interested inquiry into individuals' historical and cultural backgrounds engendered by the art project and indicated a positive perspective of herself and others as diverse and different. Similarly, Mateo, a Spanish-English bilingual and Latino senior of Mexican heritage, indicated a healthy perspective of diversity.

Mateo talked particularly about the power of the artwork as representing how diverse cultures can work productively together saying, "If you view the art and see like a bunch of high schoolers with different backgrounds and from like different places, you can still see how they come together and agree on a certain subject regardless of who they are" (April 2016).

Echoing a similar healthy perspective on diversity and resistance to marginalization, Tomás stated, "I learned that basically you have to speak up for yourself and not let other people tell you who you are. And, you know, be yourself" (April 2016). Diversity symbolized a strength, not something to be overcome, for these ELL youth. According to Tomás, it was something you should author and define yourself.

Rather than being inequitably marginalized and "othered," the cultures of ELLs were showcased and celebrated along with other diverse cultures in the school community through the production of the mural. The result was the third finding: the ELL students described stronger feelings of social connectedness, particularly to their art classmates and art teachers.

Describing working as a group to negotiate different ideas into one cohesive product, as well as learning more about each person, Dahlia said,

> I loved working together and . . . the "I am . . ." statements, . . . different people and see[ing] who they are . . . looking at the different pieces of paper we wrote. . . . To put something [together when] our minds are so different but like working together to make it work. And I like the meaning behind the project—. . . speaking and standing out together. . . . I feel like we're all in this together. . . . I have a connection with Ms. Yates . . . working with her and trying to figure stuff out . . . it was crazy. . . . But I feel like we worked together to get to where we are now. (April 2016)

Mateo shared that he felt as though he connected with his classmates because "although we're all different, we all kinda have the same opinion [of] how the world changes" (April 2016). Dahlia even suggested that if the project had been restructured, then the connection to the larger school could have been stronger.

SUGGESTIONS AND RECOMMENDATIONS FOR THE P–12 PRACTITIONER

Open Dialogue, Trusting Community, and Cultural Norms

Key to a critical pedagogy of place (Gruenewald, 2003) is engaging youth in an analysis of their everyday lived experiences. The youth will be experts on their past and ongoing experiences, even if they might not yet have the language to articulate the ways in which power functions. In order for the youth to explore their experiences and develop critical lenses, there must be open dialogue between students and teachers, as well as among students.

Open dialogue first requires a strong sense of classroom community built on care and trust. This sense of community will be gradually cultivated over time. Teachers may aim to earn their students' trust by being consistent in the behaviors they demonstrate and the messages they communicate. For instance, disciplinary and classroom-management decisions should be fair, be equitable, and have a clear rationale. Even more, these decisions can be developed with input from students. Care may also be consistently demonstrated by teachers taking time to ask questions of their students about their lives or attending their extracurricular activities.

During this open dialogue, the voices and perspectives of youth should be prioritized. It is also very important to ensure safety, respect, and sensitivity for all as cultural norms during dialogue. As with disciplinary and classroom-management decisions, these cultural norms may be collaboratively determined between teachers and students. Once these cultural norms are established, the teacher will play a vital role in maintaining and reinforcing these behavioral expectations, again with consistency.

Disciplinary Connections

This activist art project took place in two collaborating art classrooms; however, with adjustments, the project can also take place in other subjects as the practice of informed argumentation transcends disciplines. In science, for instance, the current Next Generation Science Standards (NGSS) states that students are expected to develop arguments based on empirical evidence, as well as evaluate and communicate information as science and engineering practices. Furthermore, these science and engineering practices are to be based on foundational scientific concepts and phenomenon.

The critical pedagogy of place activist art project can be adapted for science by focusing student critique on science-related social and environmental justice issues, again in students' everyday experiences. As an example, the poor west-end neighborhoods of Louisville, Kentucky, that are highly populated by low-income communities of color have been identified as urban heat islands; these areas are significantly hotter than the surrounding rural areas as a result of human activity, and this effect is advancing at one of the fastest rates in the country (Louisville Metro Tree Advisory Commission, 2013; Office of Sustainability, 2016).

The disproportionately low levels of urban tree canopy as environmental resources and the disproportionately high burden of health and wellness risks on west-end residents due to living in urban heat islands are issued related to both environmental justice and science. These align with NGSS disciplinary core ideas organized under ESS3.C: Human Impacts on Earth Systems.

The activist art project can be implemented while advancing teaching and learning aligned with science education standards by focusing open dialogue on issues such as disproportionality in the distribution of environmental resources and risks across communities based on demographics such as socioeconomic status and racial and ethnic background.

The students can explore evidence of environmental justice using books, documentaries, magazine articles, and reports. Students can also conduct primary research studies, such as environmental surveys of their neighborhoods, to assess the quality of urban tree canopy, surface temperatures, or animal and plant biodiversity as measures of environmental health. As in the "I am . . ." project, the youth can then communicate an informed argument through activist art to engage and educate others.

RECOMMENDED RESOURCES

- To support youth in reflecting critically on their everyday lives and to develop and pursue research projects to support change in their local communities: Mirra, N., Garcia, A., & Morrell, E. (2015). *Doing youth participatory action research: Transforming inquiry with researchers, educators, and students.* New York: Routledge.
- To engage cogenerative dialogues for establishing ethical discourse between students and teachers: Stith, I., & Roth, W.-M. (2010). Teaching as mediation: The cogenerative dialogue and ethical understandings. *Teaching and Teacher Education, 26*(2), 363–370. doi:10.1016/j.tate.2009.09.008.
- To utilize dialogue to establish cultural norms of trust and respect: Glenview Elementary. (2014, July 1). Using dialogue circles to support classroom management. *Edutopia*. Retrieved from https://www.edutopia.org/practice/stw-glenview-practice-dialogue-circles-video.
- To understand the connections between the creative arts and STEM (science, technology, engineering, and mathematics): Maeda, J. (2012, October 2). STEM to STEAM: Art in K–12 is key to building a strong econo-

my. *Edutopia.* Retrieved from https://www.edutopia.org/blog/stem-to-steam-strengthens-economy-john-maeda.
- To integrate art into STEM with integrity for deeper, standards-based student learning: Riley, S. (2013, December 18). Pivot point: At the crossroads of STEM, STEAM and arts integration. *Edutopia.* Retrieved from https://www.edutopia.org/blog/pivot-point-stem-steam-arts-integration-susan-riley.

NOTE

I'd like to thank and recognize the tremendous work accomplished by the Seneca High School art department led by Mrs. Melissa Molohon and Mrs. Kelly Thompson, and the art students who participated in the activist art project. The project was initiated by Jeffrey Jamner and Talleri McRae of the Kentucky Center for the Performing Arts. I also graciously thank Tytianna Smith, a PhD student in curriculum and instruction at the College of Education and Human Development, University of Louisville, who supported the research efforts as a graduate research assistant.

REFERENCES

Akom, A. A., Cammarota, J., & Ginwright, S. (2008). Youthtopias: Towards a new paradigm of critical youth studies. *Youth Media Reporter, 2*(4), 1–30.

Callahan, R. M. (2005). Tracking and high school English learners: Limiting opportunity to learn. *American Educational Research Journal, 42*(2), 305–328. doi:10.3102/00028312042002305.

Callahan, R. M., & Gándara, P. (2004). On nobody's agenda: Improving English language learners' access to higher education. In M. Sadowski (Ed.), *Teaching immigrant and second-language students: Strategies for success* (pp. 107–127). Cambridge, MA: Harvard Education Press.

Campana, A. (2011). Agents of possibility: Examining the intersections of art, education, and activism in communities. *Studies in Art Education, 52*(4), 278–291. doi:10.1080/00393541.2011.11518841.

Gruenewald, D. A. (2003). The best of both worlds: A critical pedagogy of place. *Educational Researcher, 32*(4), 3–12. doi:10.3102/0013189x032004003.

Gude, O. (2007). Principles of possibility: Considerations for a 21st-century art and culture curriculum. *Art Education, 60*(1), 6–17. doi:10.2307/27696187.

Harklau, L. (2000). From the "good kids" to the "worst": Representations of English language learners across educational settings. *TESOL Quarterly, 34*(1), 35–67. doi:10.2307/3588096.

Harris, A., Wyn, J., & Younes, S. (2010). Beyond apathetic or activist youth: "Ordinary" young people and contemporary forms of participation. *Young, 18*(1), 9–32. doi:10.1177/110330880901800103.

Jefferies, J. (2008). Do undocumented students "play by the rules"? *Journal of Adolescent and Adult Literacy, 52*(3), 249–251. doi:10.1598/JAAL.52.3.8.

———. (2014). The production of "illegal" subjects in Massachusetts and high school enrollment for undocumented youth. *Latino Studies, 12*(1), 65–87. doi:10.1057/lst.2014.5.

Johnson, F. L., & Fine, M. G. (2016). The role of the press in framing the bilingual education debate: Ten years after sheltered immersion in Massachusetts. *New England Journal of Public Policy, 28*(2), 1–22.

Kanno, Y., & Kangas, S. E. N. (2014). "I'm not going to be, like, for the AP": English language learners' limited access to advanced college-preparatory courses in high school. *American Educational Research Journal, 51*(5), 848–878. doi:10.3102/0002831214544716.

Louisville Metro Tree Advisory Commission. (2013, April 23). Whitehall house and gardens meeting minutes. LouisvilleKY.gov. Retrieved from https://louisvilleky.gov.

Moran, T. T., & Petsod, D. (2003). Newcomers in the American workplace: Improving employment outcomes for low-wage immigrants and refugees. Retrieved from https://eric.ed.gov/.

Nieto, S., & Bode, P. (2012). *Affirming diversity: The sociopolitical context of multicultural education.* Boston: Pearson.

Office of Sustainability, City of Louisville. (2016). Urban heat island project. LouisvilleKy.gov. Retrieved from https://louisvilleky.gov/government/sustainability/urban-heat-island-project.

Solorzano, D. G., & Delgado Bernal, D. (2001). Examining transformational resistance through a critical race and LatCrit theory framework: Chicana and Chicano students in an urban context." *Urban Education, 36*(3), 308–342. doi:10.1177/0042085901363002.

Ulanoff, S. H., & Vega-Castaneda, L. (2003). The sociopolitical context of bilingual instruction in 21st-century California: Examining the impact of Proposition 27. Proceedings of the Hawaii International Conference on Education. Retrieved from http://hiceducation.org/conference-proceedings.

Warriner, D. S. (2007). Language learning and the politics of belonging: Sudanese women refugees becoming and being "American." *Anthropology and Education Quarterly, 38*(4), 343–359. doi:10.1525/aeq.2007.38.4.343.

Chapter Eleven

Everyday Photography Tips for Your Classroom

Destiny De La Rosa

LEADING LINES

Leading lines is for more advanced photographers who would like a challenge. This is a technique used where there are either horizontal or vertical lines leading up to a focus point. The lines usually start at the bottom of the photograph and move through the picture until it has reach the focus point.

Things to Think About

Look at the background. You want nothing distracting you from what you want to focus on. You also want to have good lighting, to be able to clearly see the lines in the photograph.

PATTERN (RHYTHMIC PATTERN)

When thinking about pattern, don't think about the rules you learned for leading lines, rule of thirds or framing. When using pattern in your photograph, there are not main "rules" to follow. The concept of patterns can go with other concepts you have already learned. You can use bird's-eye view, take a picture from a high angle, and see a pattern you might not have seen if you were taking the photograph at height level. You can also use the abstract. Patterns can get really complex as you start to develop your style for photography.

If you are a beginner you want to start off with regular patterns. This usually involves shapes, or items in which people can easily see a clear (formation) present. For more advanced photographers, you may want to break the pattern. In a photograph that uses breaking the pattern as a concept, the audience can see a clear pattern that at some point is broken by something, but this does not take away from the overall piece.

Framing

Framing is when the photographer uses another object within the photograph as a "border" around the main subject or area of focus. Why use this? This technique gives a greater emphasis to the main subject. An example of this could be a window frame that "borders" a subject. What are some things in your classroom that you can use as a border?

Symmetry

Symmetry is when you take a picture and it is the same on both sides (horizontal and vertical). To check if the picture is symmetrical, you can fold the picture in half, creating the "line of symmetry," and can see if both sides are in fact the same. This technique creates balance and has a point of interest.

Figure 11.1. Evidence of the Rule of Thirds. *Photo by Destiny DeLarosa.*

Look around your classroom and see if you can spot something that is symmetrical. Some examples could be the ceiling pattern, a road, or a football field.

Abstract

When taking pictures that are abstract, there are no rules that need to be considered. Taking abstract pictures is about having fun. Pictures that are abstract have a sense of mystery to them. It forces the audience to look at it for a longer time.

There is no one way to do this, but here are some suggestions you can think about when taking an abstract photo.

- Get really close to an object. Since you can't see the whole object in the frame, then it could be seen as abstract.
- Have different shapes and types of textures in one photo.

Bird's-Eye View

Bird's-eye view is when you take a picture from a high angle looking down. For beginners starting to use this technique, it may help if you also use leading lines in your photograph. This would allow the audience eye to focus on the main thing you are looking to capture, but it's not required. If you want a place to start, stairs are common. You can take a picture of your subject on the first floor while you are on the second floor. By taking a picture using this perspective, you might be able to see patterns that would otherwise not have been there.

Ant's-Eye View

Ant's-eye view is the opposite of bird's-eye view. Instead of taking a photograph from a very high angle, you will take from a very low angle looking up. In order to do this, you want to get low to the ground and rise up at an angle. This could be anything from the side of a building to the bottom of someone's foot.

Ant's-eye view can be used with some of the other concepts you have read about. For example, you read about leading lines. In leading lines, the lines lead to a main subject. If you also take the picture from a low angle, it can add depth and distance to your photograph. This concept is also good to use if you have a distracting background. Again looking at your background and setting is very important!

Lighting

Lighting is a complex concept that takes much practice to master. Here are a few things to consider in terms of lighting when taking a photograph.

Take a moment and think about your setting. Are you inside or outside? If you're outside, what time of day is it? Where is the sun positioned? Is it in front of the object or subject you want to photograph? Is it on the side or behind you? These are all important questions to ask before you take the picture, because it can effect how the photograph comes out.

For example, if the sun is directly in front of the subject, this may cause the subjects to squint or close their eyes instead of having more of a relaxed face. Thinking about lighting also allows you to know whether or not flash would be needed. Photographers most commonly use flash when they are inside to add more light to what could be a semidark room, in order to make sure what they are trying to capture can be seen.

Given the general guidelines mentioned above, not following the rules also creates some creative shots as well. An example can be taking a picture of your shadow. The sun is positioned directly behind you, which allows you take a picture of yourself.

Now take the time to play around with lighting in your photographs. Take into account some of the things you have read, but also break some of the rules if you want and see what you come up with.

Rule of Thirds

One of the most important concepts in photography is the *rule of thirds*. This concept acts more as a guideline to photographers for where their subject or main area of focus should be. To test the rule of thirds you want to draw two horizontal and vertical lines on the picture similar to a tick-tack-toe grid. You have now created nine equal boxes with four intersections. The idea behind the four intersections is that these are the places your eye naturally goes to when first looking at a photograph, so you want your main area of focus to be at one of these points. To check if you have done this, first take into account the other concepts you have read about. Take some pictures, and draw a tick-tack-toe grid on the photo. Is your main area of focus located at any one of the four intersections?

Dominance

Using this concept is very common in photography. It can be used for a variety of shots, such as portrait where the subject is in the center and the main focus. This is commonly used with beginner photographers because we naturally want things to be centered. To achieve a photograph using this concept, you want to first consider looking at the background. For this concept it is very important that you don't have anything distracting in your background that would allow the audience to lose focus from what you are trying to capture. Some suggestions are thinking about the size. When something large is in a photograph, it tends to stand out more. Another suggestion is color—a bold color such as red can make an item stand out and thus create a focus point.

Index

Abedi, Jamal, 66
activist art project: argument made through, 109; bidirectional learning in, 110; communication pushing boundaries in, 110; community and trust establishment in, 108; critical pedagogy of place in, 107–108, 112; cultural norms in, 112; Dahlia on group work of, 111; Dahlia sharing in, 110, 110–111, 111; design of, 109–110; desired outcomes for, 108; diversity perspective of students in, 110–111; everyday lived experiences analysis in, 112; historical genocide focus of, 108; "I am . . ." statements as instructional resources in, 110; "I am . . ." statements mural of, 108–109, 109; Mateo on diverse cultures working together in, 111; open dialogue in, 112; oppression based on lived experiences in, 107; "othered" cultures celebrated in, 111; population and ELLs figures in, 107; resources for, 113–114; science adaptation and example in, 112–113; social challenges of students in, 107; social connectedness in, 111; teacher collaboration in, 108; Tomás and Hawa interaction in, 110; Tomás on diversity and resistance, 111
"Aesthetic Themes of Education" (Moroye and Uhrmacher), 5

art: Amy's common interests and shared expertise in, 45–47; Amy's story in, 39–40; collective discoveries and collaborative projects in, 45, 46; conversation and communication in, 41, 48; curriculum topic knowledge in, 43–44, 44; ELLs multiple entry points and scaffolds in, 47–48; ELLs participation and language proficiency in, 40; emergent curriculum in, 39; emotionally responsive bear curriculum in, 45–46; found objects use in, 42, 44, 48; hands-on explorations in, 42, 43, 48; inquiry-based curriculum in, 39; language scaffolding in, 40; materials study in, 42; "messing about" table in, 42; mural painting collaboration in, 45; open-ended activities in, 41, 48; ownership of space in, 40; paper-making activity in, 47; self-portraits use in, 42; sense of belonging activities for, 41; social and linguistic development in, 40; social justice and positive change advancement in, 106; tree sculpture activity in, 44; tree study in, 42–44; as universally accessible medium, 40; vocabulary use in, 40, 42, 43, 44; whole-class experiences in, 41; youth sociopolitical issues interest through, 106–107. *See also* project arts-based learning

Art as Experience (Dewey), 3
arts integration: Art Week expression of learning in, 20; atelier use in, 18, 19; community arts partners and artists in, 2; in curriculum, 2–3; desert habitat questioning example in, 24–25; group work in, 21; iterative group work in, 22–23; learning wall in, 20; pedagogy of participation in, 21, 28; questioning and vocabulary scaffolding in, 22–23; questioning as assessment in, 24–25; Reggio Emilia approach and classroom design in, 18; science and social studies unit in, 18–19; science unit sound example in, 23; sensemaking through, 17–18, 23–24; sheltered language instruction protocol in, 1; sketchbook use in, 19–20; small group exploration of provocations in, 20; student misconception of pollination example in, 25–27, 26; T4T implications and recommendations in, 27–28; T4T oral language development in, 22; T4T warehouse trips in, 18
assessment: arts integration questioning as, 24–25; e-portfolios as tool in, 83, 92, 93; performance-based, 85–86

Baryshnikov, Mikhail, 61
Because (Baryshnikov and Radunsky), 61
Blockhead, the Life of Fibonacci (D'Agnese), 67
Brett, Jan, 67
Buck, Gayle, 52

C3. *See* College, Career, and Civic Life Social Studies Framework
Call Me Tree (Gonzalez), 44
CCSS. *See* Common Core State Standards
C.L.A.W. homework menu: CRISPA use in, 9, 11; fifth-grade student project using, 9, 12; power of choice in, 13; second-and-third grade parent involvement with, 12
close photo observation lesson, photography: detailed photo "wonder" or "notice" in, 33; game of, 34; skill and vocabulary enhancement in, 34; unrelated photo use in, 34

cognitive apprenticeship: components of, 3; in imagination, 5
Cohn, Diana, 65
College, Career, and Civic Life (C3) Social Studies Framework, 19
Common Core State Standards (CCSS), 102
connections, 111; ELLs importance of, 4; SIOP model in, 4; student and content, 4
Connections, Risk-taking, Imagination, Sensorial experiences, Perceptivity, and Active engagement (CRISPA), 2, 5, 14; aesthetic experience dimensions of, 3–4; aesthetic overlay of, 2; C.L.A.W. homework menu use of, 9, 11; ELLs engagement in, 1, 5–6, 13; first-grade community traditions project using, 6–10, 7; fourth-grade genius hour project using, 8, 10–11; research on, 3; suggestions and recommendations for use of, 13–14
Cook, Kristin, 52
Cordova, Amy, 65
CRISPA. *See* Connections, Risk-taking, Imagination, Sensorial experiences, Perceptivity, and Active engagement
critical dialogues, 69, 74, 77
critical pedagogy of place, 107–108, 112
Cummins, Jim, 60

D'Agnese, Joseph, 67
daily fun fact lesson, photography: dolphin example in, 32; positive peer interaction in, 33; strange fact use in, 32; subject areas in, 33; truth in, 33; weekly fact use in, 33; wonder wall use in, 33
Dewey, John, 3
Dream Carver (Cohn and Cordova), 65
Duncan, Isadora, 61

ELLs. *See* English language learners
emotionally responsive bear curriculum, 45–46
English language learners (ELLs), 74; active engagement of, 1, 5–6, 13; art as multiple entry points and scaffolds for, 47–48; art participation and language proficiency of, 40; character-based

Index

assumptions about, 106; cognitive apprenticeship components for, 3; collaboration and group work with, 4–5, 21; connections importance to, 4; CRISPA use with, 1, 13; critical dialogues use for, 69; demographic change in, 59; as emergent bilingual students, 17; e-portfolios connection on development of, 84; identity support for, 106; imagination use with, 5; limited language proficiency of, 1; marginalization of, 105, 111; minimal expectations in education and careers of, 105; oppressive ideologies and institutional barriers to opportunities for, 106; pedagogy of participation for, 21, 28; perceptivity in knowledge acquisition of, 5; performance-based assessments supporting, 85–86; photography as language barrier aid to, 29; photography oral and written literacy skills development of, 53, 58; photography participation of, 29; photography use benefit to, 35; photovoice connection to language development for, 79–81; questions modeling of, 43; risk-taking safe spaces for, 4; schools bi-or multilingual education limitation of, 105–106; sense of belonging activities for, 41; sensory experience of, 5; SIOP use with, 3; student population of, 3, 51, 59, 83, 96, 107; visuals as power for, 103. *See also specific topics*

e-portfolios, 94; artifact reflection template for, 88, 91; artistic identity development in, 83, 84, 84–85; as authentic assessment tools, 83, 92, 93; cross-curricular learning in, 86–87; curriculum expectations as guide in, 88; ELLs development connection in, 84; formatting choices in, 86; image significance in, 86–87; implementation questions for, 93; LTP use in, 85; metacognition link of, 84; as performance-based assessments, 85; platforms for, 93; process-based type of, 86; process of learning emphasis in, 85, 85–86; reflection in, 84, 85, 87; self-assessment tasks in, 87; set structure for, 88; short biography use in, 87; SRL in, 87–88, 91; student learning support examples for, 91–92; student-selected artifacts in, 86–87; Suzy's vignette using, 83–84, 91; Suzy's written reflection example in, 88–89, 89; technological advantages in, 84; Tom's biography example in, 90, 90–91; tools for, 86; wide range of material use in, 84

Faltis, Christian, 66
first-grade community traditions project: CRISPA graphic organizer and lesson sketch use in, 6, 7; CRISPA use in, 6; lesson description of, 6–8; risk-taking in, 6; SIOP in, 6; student empathy example in, 6–8; student talking in, 6; teachers tips in, 8–10; vocabulary journal use in, 8
fourth-grade genius hour project: brainstorming activity in, 10; CRISPA elements in, 10; CRISPA graphic organizer and student project in, 8; lesson description of, 10–11; student research in, 10; teacher tips on, 11; vocabulary list in, 10–11
Freire, Paulo, 51, 70–71

Gardner, Howard, 2
Gibbons, Pauline, 6
Gonzalez, Maya, 44
Grandfather Tang's Story (Tompert), 63
group work, 4–5; of activist art project, 111; in arts integration, 20, 21, 22–23; in photovoice, 79; in project arts-based learning, 61, 64, 65; in seasons lesson, photography, 30

hands-on explorations: in art, 42, 43, 48; in project arts-based learning, 62
How the Brain Learns (Sousa), 2
"I am . . ." statements mural, 108–109, 109

imagination: cognitive apprenticeship method in, 5; ELLs use of, 5
inquiry-based curriculum, 39, 59

Klee, Paul, 64
Koplow, Leslie, 45–46
Kroeger, Steve, 52

Lange, Dorothea, 52
language acquisition, 1–2, 4, 59, 79
learning wall, 20
linguistically responsive teaching (LRT), 66
literacy, 51–52, 53, 58, 81
literacy through photography (LTP), 85
LRT. *See* linguistically responsive teaching
LTP. *See* literacy through photography
Lucas, Tamara, 66

McCloud, Scott, 97, 103
The Mitten (Brett), 67
Molohon, Melissa, 109
Moroye, Christy, 5
Multiple Intelligences (Gardner), 2

Next Generation Science Standards (NGSS), 19, 112, 113

O'Brien, John, 67
One Tree (Tabler), 44
open dialogue, 112
oral language development, 22, 53, 58, 63, 102

paper-making activity, 47
pedagogy of participation, 21, 28
photography: abstract photo in, 119; after-school program in, 51–52, 53, 55; ant's-eye view use in, 119; background in, 117; beginning class in, 55–56; bird's-eye view use in, 119; camera donations for, 56; close photo observations in, 33–34; daily fun fact lesson in, 32–33; dominance concept in, 120; ELLs benefit of using, 35; ELLs language barrier aid of, 29; ELLs oral and written literacy skills development in, 53, 58; ELLs participation in, 29; as engagement tool, 52; evidence using in, 54; examples of uses for, 30; finger use in, 35; focus in, 53; framing as border in, 118; gallery space use in, 57; leading lines in, 117; lighting concept in, 120; literacy and, 51–52; memory cards and batteries purchase for, 56–57; microaggressions addressed in, 56; narrative inquiry in, 52; patterns in, 117–118; perspective taking in, 54, 55; photo elicitation research in, 29; photovoice use in, 52; portrait viewing and questions in, 53–54; positive learning environment in, 35–36; rule of thirds in, 120; seasons lesson in, 30–31; storytelling with, 54; student identity reclaiming in, 57–58; symmetry in, 118–119; "think time" in, 35; vocabulary building in, 54; weather impacting, 57; writing prompts in, 34
photovoice, 52, 70, 81; audio recorder use in, 74, 80; brochure for, 73; content and language objectives addressed in, 69; critical dialogues use in, 74; critical reflection in, 75–76; critical theory and pedagogy origins of, 70; ELLs connection to language development in, 79–81; feminist theory in, 71; findings sharing in, 75; Freire approach in, 70–71; funds of knowledge use in, 80; informed consent and permission use in, 72–73; key aims of, 70; participatory action research methodology of, 69, 71, 75; personal and community change in, 70; personal narrative use in, 75; picture taking and sharing decisions in, 73; planning for, 71; practice session of, 73; research skills and critical thinking in, 70; safety issue in, 72; shared decision making in, 71; SHOWeD method questions for, 74–75; situations or concerns addressed in, 73; small group discussion in, 79; social and environmental injustice issues in, 70, 71; spoken and written language combining in, 74; student introduction to, 72; visual data analysis in, 75; visual literacy development in, 81; writing and reading comprehension in, 80; YPAR use in, 71
photovoice, Wellington, New Zealand: audio recorders use in, 78; photo elicitation activity of, 77, 78; program

overview of, 76; purpose of, 76; science, environmental literacy and social justice connection in, 76, 78, 79; short paragraph writing in, 77–78; SHOWeD questions for critical dialogue in, 77; stormwater understanding in, 76, 77; student-friendly handout use in, 76–77; student pairing in, 77

professional development workshops, 3, 66–67

project arts-based learning: action verb use in, 61; *Because* as visual model in, 61; bilingual students and, 59–60; "Can Do Descriptors" in, 60; *Dream Carver* story use in, 65; engagement and collaboration in, 59; framework for, 67; group work and partnering in, 61, 64, 65; hands-on strategies use in, 62; humanizing effect of, 67; language learning framework in, 60; LRT use in, 66; math lesson on measuring space as, 62–63; math lesson on pricing clay toys as, 65, 66; oral language production in, 63; outcome of, 61–62; pipe cleaner and wood sculptures in, 62, 63; pride of ownership in, 67; professional development workshops on, 66–67; real-world financial decisions in, 65; school ambiance in, 60; shadow puppet lesson and objective in, 61–62, 62; as student-centered pedagogy, 59; tangram use in mathematical learning as, 63–64; translanguaging use in, 60

Radunsky, Vladimir, 61
Redwood-Jones, Yanique, 73
reflection, 84; in e-portfolios, 84, 85, 87, 88, 88–89, 89, 91; in photovoice, 75–76; in Selfie Project, 99–100
risk-taking, 6; collaboration and group work in, 4–5; ELLs safe spaces for, 4; SIOP interaction with, 5

science, 76, 78, 79; activist art project adaptation and example of, 112–113; arts integration unit and sound example in, 18–19, 23

seasons lesson, photography: journal work in, 30; photo comparison in, 30, 31, 32; student photo job in, 31; whole group observation and discussion in, 30

selfie: curricular use of, 95, 102; first documented, 95; genres of writing use of, 102; oral presentation use of, 102; research and pedagogy of, 95; uses of, 95

Selfie Project: comic book basis of, 96–97; creation of, 96; detail adding in, 99, 101; final edit and reflection in, 99–100; flow and recall in, 100–101, 101; implementation steps of, 98, 99; intersecting combination use in, 97; picture-specific combination use in, 97; portable electronic device use in, 98; reflective writing assignment in, 98; reflective writing words emergence in, 100; scavenger hunt and answer sharing in, 98–99; self-awareness of writer in, 98, 100, 101; selfie-taking task approaches in, 101; six areas of writing in, 99; two-panel story in, 97; visual cues in, 101; word and picture combinations in, 97; writing project on community as, 98; writing stories with and without selfie in, 99

Selfie Researchers Network, 95
self-portraits, 42
self-regulated learning (SRL) theory, 87–88, 91
sense of belonging activities, 41
sensory experience: cultural product use in, 5; ELLs sense of belonging in, 5; varied ways of understanding by using, 5
shadow puppet lesson, 61–62, 62
sheltered language instruction protocol, 1, 11, 14; arts integration in, 1–2; professional development in, 3
Sheltered Observation Instructional Protocol (SIOP): components of, 3; connections in, 4; ELLs use of, 3; in First-grade community traditions project, 6; in risk-taking, 5; smaller features of, 3
SHOWeD method questions, 74–75, 77
SIOP. *See* Sheltered Observation Instructional Protocol

Sousa, David, 2
SRL. *See* self-regulated learning theory
Switzer, Sharon, 52

T4T. *See* Trash for Teaching
Tabler, Mary, 44
teacher tips: in first-grade community traditions project, 8–10; on fourth-grade genius hour project, 11; on photo elicitation, 35–36; on photography, 117–120
Thompson, Kelly, 109
Title I school, 1, 2, 39
Tompert, Ann, 63
translanguaging, 60
Trash for Teaching (T4T), 18; arts integration implications and recommendations in, 27–28; concept illustration use of, 17; oral language development using, 22; third-grade student use of, 17; warehouse trips to, 18
tree sculpture activity, 44

Uhrmacher, Bruce, 5
urban heat islands, 112–113
urban tree canopy, 113

van der Veen, Jatila, 97
Van Der Zee, James, 52
Villegas, Ana Maria, 66
vocabulary, 34; arts integration scaffolding of, 22–23; art use of, 40, 42, 43, 44; First-grade community traditions project journal use for, 8; Fourth-grade genius hour project list use of, 10–11; photography building of, 54
Vygotsky, Lev, 48

Wang, Caroline, 71, 73
WIDA. *See* World Class Instructional Design and Assessment
wonder wall, 33
World Class Instructional Design and Assessment (WIDA), 60
writing prompts, photography: chosen photo stories in, 34; creative thinking in, 34; verbal and written stories in, 34

youth participatory action research (YPAR), 71

Zenkov, Kristien, 29
zone of proximal development, 48

About the Editors and Contributors

Tabitha Dell'Angelo is associate professor at the College of New Jersey and holds a PhD in interdisciplinary studies in human development from the University of Pennsylvania. In 2009 she launched the Urban Education Program at the College of New Jersey, which is focused on recognizing and responding to conditions that contribute to inequities in schools. Over the years she has worked on large- and small-scale program evaluation as well as consulting on projects aimed at working with underserved communities to create positive change. She is also a playwright and storyteller and uses arts-based methods including photography and ethno-drama in her teaching and research. In addition, she conducts workshops on using yoga and mindfulness in classrooms and holds a RYT 500 (yoga credential).

Louise Ammentorp, PhD, is associate professor in the Department of Elementary and Early Childhood Education at the College of New Jersey. Her research interests include school-university collaboration in teacher preparation and best practices in early childhood and elementary education, in particular, arts-based curriculum and outdoor education.

Lauren Madden, PhD, is associate professor at the College of New Jersey and holds a PhD in science education from North Carolina State University. She is an elementary science and environmental educator and coordinates a five-course minor in environmental sustainability education. Her research and teaching often utilize photo-based methods to situate and provide context for teaching and learning. Her interests include science teacher development, environmental education for preservice teachers, teachers' scientific and environmental identities, and children's perceptions of nature.

About the Editors and Contributors

Jennifer D. Adams is associate professor at the University of Calgary, where she holds a dual appointment in the Department of Chemistry and the Werklund School of Education. Her research focuses on the intersection of creativity and STEM teaching and learning in postsecondary contexts. She has expertise in STEM teaching and learning in informal science contexts, including museums and national parks. She was awarded a National Science Foundation Early Career Award to study informal learning contexts and formal and informal collaborations for STEM teacher education. Her research portfolio also includes youth learning and identity in informal science contexts, with a focus on underrepresented youth and place and identity in transnational communities and environmental education.

Michelle Allen, MA, is a kindergarten teacher at PS 125, the Ralph Bunche School in New York City. She has worked in a variety of settings as both an early childhood educator and an arts specialist.

Marissa E. Bellino is assistant professor of education at the College of New Jersey (TCNJ) where she teaches social foundations and science methods to preservice teachers. Her teaching interests include environmental sustainability and science education through a critical lens. Marissa's research interests explore youth experiences in urban environments, environmental education, and participatory research.

Destiny De La Rosa is currently pursuing a master's in counseling at the College of New Jersey. She took her first photography class her sophomore year in high school, and her interest has grown ever since. She has taken all types of pictures; however, her favorite thing to photograph is nature.

Laura Felleman Fattal, PhD, is associate professor at William Paterson University in Wayne, New Jersey. Her expertise is in arts integration in the elementary K–6 classroom. She is widely published in the areas of art education, visual literacy, visual culture, and bilingualism and the arts. Fattal is a frequent presenter at national and regional educational conferences.

Rebecca Garte holds a PhD in developmental psychology. She is assistant professor in the teacher education department of the Borough of Manhattan Community College of the City University of New York. Her research interests are on the factors affecting academic outcomes among low-income populations across school contexts.

Donna Goodwin, PhD, has been an art educator in all levels of K–12 and museum education, and she is a licensed teacher and principal. She is currently assistant professor of art education at the University of Northern Colorado and the visual arts content consultant for the Colorado Department of Education.

Joanna Higgins is associate professor at the Faculty of Education, Victoria University of Wellington, New Zealand. Her areas of interest include teacher professional inquiry in mathematics, the design of professional learning and development, and student learning environments.

Maureen Hudson graduated from the College of New Jersey in 2017 with a degree in elementary education and integrative STEM with a biology specialization. She is currently pursuing her master's in urban education and TESL certification at TCNJ. Her research interests include peace and contemplative education, culturally responsive teaching practices, and social-emotional development of young children. In the future, she hopes to serve as an elementary educator and educational researcher with a focus on teaching to the whole child—body, mind, and spirit.

Sheron L. Mark, PhD, is assistant professor of science education at the University of Louisville. She focuses on nontraditional instructional methods, including art, as means to enhance youth's experiences and learning environments. She approaches art as a vehicle for activism to support youth voice, sense of belonging, and resistance.

Sarah Morrison, PhD, is curriculum chair of the visual and performing arts department at Appleby College in Oakville, Ontario, adjunct instructor at Queen's University in Kingston, and artistic director of the Oakville Children's Choir. She is known for her energy and creativity in working with young voices. Her research interests focus on technology-enhanced learning environments, collaborative community singing, and innovation in arts education.

Carissa Natalewicz has been a first-grade teacher at Ben Franklin Elementary School in Lawrenceville, New Jersey, for the last three years. She graduated from the College of New Jersey in 2013 with a degree in early childhood education/psychology.

Browning Neddeau, MA, EdD, is assistant professor of education in the liberal studies department at California State University, Monterey Bay. His research is centered on arts education, agriculture education, and the culturally appropriate representation of Native Americans in schools.

Kristin Papoi is clinical assistant professor at the University of North Carolina at Chapel Hill. Her doctoral research at the University of Wisconsin,

Madison, focused on the affordances of arts-based pedagogies for English language learners. She taught grades 3–5 in Los Angeles where she served as her school's arts coordinator.

P. Bruce Uhrmacher, PhD, is professor of research methods and education at the Morgridge College of Education, University of Denver. His areas of interest include arts-based research and aesthetic orientations to teaching and learning.

www.ingramcontent.com/pod-product-compliance
Lightning Source LLC
Chambersburg PA
CBHW021852300426
44115CB00005B/121